T0165263

A RANT AND A ROAD TRIP

JOURNAL 2009

BRENDAN J. A. O'LEARY

iUNIVERSE, INC.
NEW YORK   BLOOMINGTON

A Rant and a Road Trip
Journal 2009

iUniverse books may be ordered through booksellers or by contacting:

iUniverse
1663 Liberty Drive
Bloomington, IN 47403
www.iuniverse.com
1-800-Authors (1-800-288-4677)

Because of the dynamic nature of the Internet, any Web addresses or links contained in this book may have changed since publication and may no longer be valid.

ISBN: 978-1-4502-7325-1 (sc)
ISBN: 978-1-4502-7326-8 (ebk)

Printed in the United States of America

iUniverse rev. date: 4/5/2011

INTRODUCTION

Before you start reading my meagre contribution to the world of literature, there are a few points I'd like to make.

This is not a book. Well, not in the conventional sense.

Although I have now made nine road trips, this is only my fourth attempt at writing about my travels. My first attempt (2006) was pitiful to say the least, and with all the skilled help in the world would never be good enough to see the light of day.

Though the following two attempts saw a marked improvement in my writing, it is doubtful (though not impossible) that they will ever surface either.

Perhaps I'm being too hard on myself, allowing my insecurities to cloud my judgement.

It's possible.

Very possible, in fact.

What you must understand, before joining me on my little jaunt, is that this is nothing more than a daily account of a holiday/road trip that I took during 2009. And, though my style of writing and use of language may, at times, appear alien to those of you who live *'across the pond',* as you like to say in America, I trust that this will not prove to be too much of an imposition. Good show. I aim to please.

To me, it is simply ludicrous to think that an individual (even a professional writer) could possibly write a book in a mere 37 days. Therefore, I ask only that you see this simple piece of writing for what it is: A journal.

Someone once told me that it took Joseph Heller seven years to write Catch 22. So then. Were I to take a seven year road trip, and come up with one book, why, I'm pretty damn sure that it would be far better than what lies in store for you here today.

Had I started keeping detailed accounts of my road trips from the year 2000 onwards, and then perhaps added a little fiction here and there, just to spice things up as it were, I would have sufficient material by now for something resembling a half decent book. But I didn't, and I haven't, so this will have to suffice.

Writing is not something that comes naturally to me. In fact, at school I absolutely hated English. As for reading, well, books were just boring, positively boring. However, things are different now. I'm different now. And, I count myself lucky that I have found something that, although I'm still very much a novice, I'm getting better at all the time. Yes. It's true what they say, you know *'It's never too late'*.

Though I can't give you an exact figure, I should say that I have only read 70-80 books in my life. Had I read more in my formative years, I may well have been a better writer. I'll never know.

As you make your way through the pages of this journal, at whatever pace you desire, you will notice I occasionally make reference to the previous year's journal (2008). However, you now know not to go looking for it, as it doesn't exist, well not in published form, though as I alluded to earlier, it *may* see the light of day, as *may* its predecessor, the 2007 journal.

For now, however, I am only interested in making the most of this journal, and also, focusing on my next literary contribution, journal 2010.

Though it was never my intention to have any of my journals published, I agreed to do so when those closest to me who had read them, convinced me that this particular one was indeed worthy of publication. At first I was sceptical, but eventually came to the conclusion that I had nothing to lose.

Of course, what those closest to me and the general public think could well be two different things.

And then there are the cultural differences. Although I am travelling and writing about my experiences in America, the American public may hate my work. Likewise, the readers in England may very well hate it too. Yes. It's a minefield, and no mistake. But I shall press on. Sink or swim, I must see it through to the end. I must steel myself for criticism from all sides. Anyway. Didn't someone once say, *'there's no such thing as bad publicity.'*? I believe they did.

Now, at this point, you may well be asking yourself these two questions: *'What's different about this book and the style of writing, compared to any other travel related book?'* and, *'what makes it original?'* and my answer would have to be, *'I don't profess to be different or original, it has simply become my mission (hopefully) to entertain.'*

Although there is no guarantee that my first foray into the world of writing will be a success, nevertheless, I shall endeavour to write more and, I believe, better prose.

You will notice (though you may not care), that there are no chapters in this book/journal, but how can there be? As I have already said, it is merely a day by day account of a road trip and, in my opinion, there simply isn't any need for them.

Several months after this journal was completed, and shortly before writing the introduction, I was given a copy of *'On the Road',* by the legendary Jack Kerouac. Though I found it hard going, not least because of the unusual language he used, nevertheless, it *was* interesting. Although the names were fictional, the characters were based on real people, which fascinated me. However, although the book itself was a great success (in terms of sales), and made Kerouac a household name, the failure by the general public to understand exactly what it was about, would cause Kerouac much distress and probably lead to his untimely death in 1969, at the age of just 47. Tragic.

Long after Kerouac's death I saw a television interview, in which he got very angry with the young people in the audience, who looked upon him as some kind of rebel leader. Or, as they put it: *'Godfather of the beat movement'.* To them he was saying: *'Go where you want to go. Do what you want to do. Be what you want to be. Let tomorrow take care of itself, and let others* (the older generation) *do the worrying.'* But they were wrong. Kerouac's road trips were all to do with spirituality. He was constantly searching for something. Ah! But this now begs the question: Did he find what he was looking for? To answer that question, one would have to know exactly what it was that he was seeking. Sadly, we will never know, though I think it's safe to say that he wanted a closer relationship with God.

After completing the difficult task of reading *'On the Road',* I got to thinking about my own road trips, and started wondering whether there was anything spiritual about them. Was I looking for something? Was I trying to find God? Was I trying to find, and better understand myself? Oh, I don't know. However, I'll tell you this. In 2008 I wrote three poems, one of which was entitled *'The Lonely Traveller'.* This particular poem starts off thus: *'I'm looking for something, I'm hoping to find, a person, a place, or just peace of mind,'* So then. Maybe to some degree, my road trips are of a spiritual nature.

Will I ever find what I'm looking for? Who can say? (Cue U2)

Just for the record, I would like to make it perfectly clear that I do not compare myself to Kerouac in any way. Far from it, in fact. He was a highly intelligent man, a genius. I, on the other hand, am merely an amateur. If this book/journal fails to live up to your expectation, what can I say? I did my best.

Finally, I should like to take this opportunity to warn you that I do have a tendency to talk about food rather a lot, but then, as it was never my intention to have this work published, don't expect an apology. However, should I decide to have any future journals published, I will most certainly learn from the mistakes made in this one.

As for the photos, I was in two minds about including them or not, but in the end decided that it would probably make for a more interesting read.

Enjoy.

DEDICATION:

For Carol MacLaren. The lady who convinced me that I really am worthy.

ACKNOWLEDGEMENTS:

Ged Kelly. Without who's help and computing skills, this task may never have been completed.

Also, several members of the Mullan family and my sister, Judith.

Manchester Airport. A place I am familiar with. Now, although I do quite like airports, I have absolutely no idea what they think of me. Hm. Do you think it might be worth asking one of them…… one day……perhaps? No. Probably not a good idea. I mean, what if an airport were to say that it didn't like me, what then? It could traumatise me so much that I might never fly again. *Then* what would I write about?

To say I got here early would be an understatement. Not that I'm complaining. After all, it's far better to arrive early than late. My driver was a nice enough chap called Jimmy, and though he talked incessantly about anything and everything, to be perfectly honest I couldn't have cared less. It was holiday time, and I was headed for the U S of A. Yes. Time for another magical mystery tour, my friends.

Jimmy arrived at my house bang on 5:00am and managed to get me to Manchester airport by 5:55am (a distance of about 50 miles). Now, you have to admit, that's pretty good going. Having said that, the roads *were* relatively quiet.

Last year, I had far more thoughts going around inside my head than I could possibly hope to put down on paper. This year I feel drained, I don't even feel particularly happy. I'm not saying that I feel sad. No. I guess I don't really feel anything. But how can this be? *Surely,* I must have *some* feelings.

'Oh, to be in England, now that summer's here.' There again, if it's summer in England, wouldn't I be better off in sunnier climes? Yes. I know. I've written that before. But where? Oh memory, why dost thou desert me in my hour of need? Oh yes. Very Shakespearean.

Never mind memory, a soupçon of inspiration is what I need right now.

Just for a change, this year I decided to take advantage of the executive lounge facilities. It's quiet. However, though it does make it much easier for me to write, with so few bodies around, I am unable to do my usual people-watching, which, as you know, is where I get most of my material. That said, although people-watching can be a fascinating pastime, for the most part, people bore me. Am I *really* human. I mean, 100 per cent human? Or, am I part alien? If so, how much of me *is* alien? Confusion reigns. Still. Makes a change from cats and dogs, eh? I'm wasted here. I should be on the telly.

Speaking of telly, GMTV is on. Ah! Penny Smith. Now, I've always fancied her. I can't say why exactly, there's just something about her, if you know what I mean.

Did I ever tell you that you should never write whilst watching telly? Well, you know what they say: *'Do as I say, don't do as I do'*.

TV. Television. Telly. Nope. This English language will always be a bloody mystery to me.

7:45am. We'll be boarding in 55 minutes, so I guess I'd better go and find out where the gate is. *Gate! Gate! wherefore art thou, gate?* Oh no, there's that bloody Shakespeare again.

Sorry about that. I got sidetracked. Now, what was it that I wanted to say? Ah, yes. As I arrived at the airport so early (5:55am) I was first in the queue. *Well?* Oh, I'm so sorry that it wasn't more interesting. Just remember, this is therapy for *me*, not *you*. If you don't like it, you don't have to read it. See if I care.

And without so much as a backward glance, he was gone.

Wednesday October 14th

Oh, woe is me!

First off, it's 2:00am on Wednesday morning, but as it's still the middle of the night for me, let's just pretend that it's still Tuesday. Hey! Whose journal is this? I make the fucking rules. Okay?

Now where were we?

I'll be honest with you, I'm not feeling at all happy, though I know not why. Consequently, I may just abandon this journal without warning. Yes. I *am* getting stressed about it. But, I did say to myself (yesterday afternoon), that if I just wanted to enjoy my holiday, then that would be precisely what I'd do.

Although I admire Stephen Fry, as far as being a writer goes, I could never ever be anywhere near as good as him at all this literary shit. Still. Each to his own, as they say.

Am I getting a cold? My nose was running all day yesterday, and it still feels a little odd today. Having said that, I feel alright.

Well, as flights go......it went......very slowly...... *AAAAAAARGH!* Oh, how I hate to fly. Still. It's just a means to an end, is it not? Yes? Well, I'm glad we're all in agreement on that.

Both my flights (Manchester to Newark, and Newark to Nashville) took off and landed on time, though for the second year running, I found myself having to go through two security checks at Newark. First, when I arrived at Terminal C, and again after I got off the shuttle train that took me from Terminal C to Terminal A. But now, *yes now,* I've discovered that after clearing the security checks at Terminal C (where they ask/tell you to take off your hat, your coat, your shoes, your belt, remove your laptop from its protective case and put all your worldly goods into those plastic boxes, which are then put through the scanner, and then walk through a metal detector frame, before being physically searched) I can simply get a shuttle bus over to Terminal A, walk up the stairs and step straight into the departure lounge. Oh, what fun. We simply must do this more often. This jet-setting lifestyle isn't all it's cracked up to be.

On the flight from Manchester to Newark I was sat next to a young couple, who, after spending the best part of seven and a half hours flying to Newark, were then going to spend a further eight hours flying to Hawaii. Had that been me, they would have had to carry me off in a straightjacket by the time I reached Hawaii

Oh, how I miss the old days, when I still drank and you could smoke on board an aircraft.

Wait a minute. If I'm having so much trouble sleeping, why am I sat here drinking a French Vanilla Coffee? Ah. It's so sweet, and creamy, and vanilla-ey (vanilla-ey?) and kind of caramely and syrupy. Did I mention yummy? Well, you get the picture. Unfortunately, you don't get the taste. Ha ha!

It does annoy me so, when this infernal contraption puts red wiggly lines under words that don't exist. Yes! Mister Computer. It's called irony. If computers are so fucking clever, then why don't they do irony? One day, someone will invent a computer with a sense of humour. Modern technology? Bah! Humbug!

It's raining outside. Well of course it's raining outside. It could hardly be raining inside, could it? No…………unless, of course, the roof were leaking. Oh shut up. Now you're just being silly. That said, I do love the sound of rain. It does have a calming effect, don't you find?

Yep. It was absolutely bucketing down when we landed in Nashville. And, although it took little more than ten minutes to get from the aircraft to the baggage carousel and then down to the car hire company (Avis), that was when my troubles began. Oh, sure. I got a car. And a good one at that. In fact, it was an old favourite, a Chevrolet Cobalt, to be precise. This is my third 'Chevy' (as they are affectionately known). But, all was not well. Yes, the car was booked and paid for. And yes, I could have it for 37 days. However, the travel company, in its infinite wisdom, had, for reasons known only to themselves, split the booking into two parts. (Effectively, two bookings.) The first booking meant that I could have the car from October 13th to November 1st, and then, the second booking would be from November 1st to November 19th. Basically, Avis wanted me to return the vehicle on November 1st and check it out again on the same day. I argued that, although I had no idea where I would be on November 1st, I certainly didn't plan to be anywhere near Nashville. *"But it's not our fault,"* the lady kept saying. *"It's the fault of the travel company."* Anyway, she did finally come up with a solution to the problem, which was for me to phone my travel service, explain the situation to them and get them to phone Avis and change the booking, thus allowing me to keep the car for the full 37 days, without interruption. And that folks, is what I'm going to do now. What a fucking performance. Of course, one could always argue that, if nothing bad ever happened, or, if nothing ever went wrong in life, we would never fully appreciate the *good* and the *right*. What a load of bollocks.

It's 5:30am, so it's still dark outside. In fact, it won't be light for at least another hour and a half. I hate driving in the dark (I also hate driving in the rain), but I'm going to head straight for the airport and get this mess sorted out. Wish me luck.

Well. What a day! I phoned the travel company in England and explained to them why I would have to return my rental car to Avis, in Nashville, on November 1st. *"No problem."* The lady said. *"I'll phone the office in Nashville and then, all you have to do is go in and sign the new rental agreement."* Yeah. And, oh look, there's a flying pig. No problem, my arse. By the time I reached the airport, it still wasn't sorted. I would have got it all sorted out sooner, but as I was entering the airport, I got into the wrong lane and ended up having to stop and ask for directions back to the fucking place. How many times have I made that journey back to the airport? Seven. That's how many. And have I ever got lost, or taken a wrong turning before? No. I started to think that the Fates were against me. *'This was not going to be a good trip'*, I thought.

After more than an hour of phone call and fax exchanges (between England and America), a diplomatic crisis was averted. I finally got to sign my new rental agreement, and order was once again restored.

God was in his heaven, the rain was still bucketing down and I made it back to my motel unscathed, only to discover that I'd missed the free breakfast. Yep. If I wanted something to eat, I was going to have to pay for it..............*AAAAAAAAARGH!*

Undaunted, I set off for Farmers, which is a new eatery, and just a couple of doors from here. It's where the Sports Bar used to be. And, I have to say, it's well worth a visit. It's one of those, all-you-can-eat places. In fact, it's where I had dinner last night. And what a dinner. Now, I've been in many all-you-can-eat establishments, but this place outdoes anything I've ever seen before. Man! The selection was just amazing. What's more, they even do the an all-you-can-eat breakfast, for the paltry sum of $9.75. Hell! Dinner only cost me $11.94, and I had two big plates of food, lemon meringue pie and a coke. Yep. I'll be going back there alright.

After breakfast, I came back to the motel and went to bed for three hours. Well, I only managed a couple of hours sleep last night, so I was really tired.

Today's been quiet. All I did was call in at *'Pay Less Shoe Source'*, to see my friend Cathy. Unfortunately, she wasn't there, but I had a good, long chat with Amanda, a young lady I got talking to this time last year.

Ah! Now I nearly forgot. I actually got to speak to Stella today (something, unfortunately, I didn't manage to do last year). I was hoping to go up and see her and Orville, either today, or tomorrow, but it's not convenient, as neither of them is too well. Never mind. Stella *did* say to give her a call after I got back from my road trip. So, if they're feeling any better, I shall take the short drive up to Sylvia Road to see them both. Oh, I do hope that they are both well enough. They're such good people. But wait a minute. Just *who are* Stella and Orville? Ah! They would be Trudy's parents. At a guess, I would say they are both about 60, though it's not the done thing to ask, is it? Oh! I'm so sorry. I neglected to tell you who Trudy is. Ah! Trudy. Dear Trudy. Trudy is a good friend of mine, and a lady I met when I first stayed in this town (Dickson, Tennessee), back in 2001.

Back then, I guess Trudy was what you'd call a chambermaid at The Eye Motel, which is just a stone's throw from Interstate 40. Now, however, with her small team of helpers, she practically runs the place. Quite a woman, and no mistake. She works all the hours God sends, and then some. Now, although I have no idea who owns the place, or what their financial situation is for that matter, I *do* believe that Trudy should be given a substantial pay increase. Not that my opinion counts for much, you understand.

I've only stayed at the Eye Motel once, in all the years I've been coming here. Sadly, it's not the smartest of places. In fact, it's rather rundown and neglected. But then, these older Mom and Pop type places find it increasingly difficult to compete with the large chains that have spread, like wildfire, right across America. They can't afford to provide a free breakfast for their patrons, nor an indoor swimming pool, exercise room (which some of them *do* have), or even a guest laundry. Consequently, I now prefer to stay in more luxurious (if that's the right word) surroundings. Trudy understands. She doesn't think any less of me.

Though Trudy is a grown woman, at 32, she is still 20 years younger than me. And, although I'm pretty sure that if I were to ask her, she'd more than likely say yes to a marriage proposal, I just can't see myself being married to anyone.

Okay! Maybe one day I'll regret it. That's life.

After I left the shoe store, I called in at the motel to see Trudy. Sadly, she has a bad cold, but is still working. Her new boyfriend came in while I was there. A quiet sort, though pleasant enough. I just hope that this relationship works out for her. God knows, that woman deserves a break. Unfortunately, she's had the misfortune of attracting some real no hopers in her life. (Mistake. He's not her boyfriend, he's just a friend.)

8:00pm, and I've had nothing to eat since breakfast. Is it too late to eat? Should I go to Farmers again? What about a French Vanilla Coffee, and a bag of pretzels, perhaps?

Trudy told me that she finishes work at 10:00pm, so I said I'd call in at about 9:45pm for a chat. The Eye Motel is only a two minute drive from here.

What about a movie? No thanks. Nothing personal. I just don't like the taste.

Yeah. Coffee, pretzels and see what's on the box.

Super 8 Motel. Dickson, Tennessee.
This motel is run by a wonderful couple called, Vince and Mita Patel.

The Eye Motel, where Trudy works.
The restaurant does a good breakfast.

THURSDAY OCTOBER 15TH

It's 7:15am, and I just got back from having breakfast. Is that grammatically correct? How the fuck would I know? I'm just the one writing this shit, *he's* the one with the brain. Well, that's what he'd have us believe. Man, this one finger typing sure is a pain in the arse. (Or should that be, pain in the finger?)

On the right side of my computer screen, photos that I scanned into this *beast* keep appearing. I've just seen the one of Orville and Stella. Ah. That picture always makes me smile. Such wonderful people.

I actually got to have breakfast in the motel this morning, which, after yesterday's fiasco, pleased me no end. I had a bowl of Raisin Bran. (I was reliably informed by Trish, only last year, that this is what it is called, and not bran flakes with raisins, as I used to call it.) *'And who might Trish be?'* I hear you ask. Oh, she's sort of an ex-penfriend of mine.

I've had (and lost) more penfriends than Liz Taylor has had (and lost) husbands. Sometimes I upset them, and sometimes they upset me. Either way ……………oh, what does it matter anymore. *'It Doesn't Matter Any More'*, is a song by the late, great Buddy Holly and, funnily enough, Trish just happens to work at the Buddy Holly Centre, in Lubbock, Texas. Now, isn't that interesting? Oh, suit yourself.

I spent just over an hour with Trudy last night. After she'd finished her shift at the motel, she had to go and put the day's takings into the night safe. So, she got into her humongous SUV (that stands for Sports Utility Vehicle, for those of you not in the know), while I got into my little Chevy and trailed along behind, like a puppy trying to keep up with its master. The woman drives like a lunatic, but I love her…………in my own special way, of course.

After she'd taken care of business at the bank, it was time for some eats. Trudy does work very long hours, consequently, she does have unconventional eating habits.

We drove north on Highway 46 for about five miles, under the railway bridge, onto Mathis Drive and then turned left into the parking lot of Waffle House. Trudy goes there a lot, apparently. There are two Waffle Houses in this town. The other one is down by the interstate (Interstate 40), and just a short walk from where I'm staying.

I wasn't particularly hungry, even though all I'd had since breakfast was half a bag of mustard-flavoured pretzels and an FVC. (If you haven't figured that out by now, then you don't deserve to be reading this drivel.) *What am I saying?* This is the finest piece of literature ever written. Yeah. But not on *this* planet.

I plumped for the chilli with crackers, which, I have to admit, was delicious. Trudy had the omelette, with hash browns and about half a bottle of ketchup. Okay, so it wasn't *quite* that much. I had a glass of orange juice, while Trudy opted for the Coke. Trudy talked about guys, and her love life. She said that sex was overrated. I could have agreed with her, but what the fuck would I know. It's been such a long time since I had any, I couldn't possibly comment.

A week ago, Trudy sent me an email, and in it, she said that she had found someone new and was really happy. However, last night she informed me that the guy in question, was 49, and married. Now, this isn't the first time that she's got herself mixed up with a married man. Will that woman ever learn?

We left Waffle House at a little after 11:00pm. Trudy (and that beast of a vehicle she just loves so much) raced out of the parking lot, like a get-away driver on a bank job and into the night. By the time I got out, she was nowhere to be seen. I looked left and right, but there was no sign of her. I left via the Hennslee Drive exit (this is also called Highway 70), turned right onto Mathis Drive, drove under the railway bridge, onto Highway 46 and drove the five miles back to my motel, thinking and worrying about Trudy. Some days, I think I'd like to take her away from all this, and give her a better life.

Damn. 9:25am already. Still so much to do. I told Trudy that I'd call in and see her at work at about 10-00am.

Like Tuesday, I only got about three hours sleep last night. Well, that's what eating late will do for you.

I lay there in bed, just listening to the sound of the rain. Although rain doesn't usually keep me awake, I had hoped that its therapeutic qualities might just help me get back to sleep. Unfortunately, this was not the case. Looks like I'll be having a siesta this afternoon.

Hey! I went to the eye care centre on Mathis Drive yesterday, as one of the lenses had fallen out of my glasses. (Actually, one of those little screws had managed to work itself loose, thus causing the lens to fall out.) I had thought about trying to repair it myself, using a little penknife I always bring with me, but then thought better of the idea, as, had I dropped the screw on the carpet, it would have been like trying to find a needle in a haystack. So, after explaining the situation to the optometrist, she very kindly repaired it, for free. Now wasn't that good of her? It's things like that that really restore one's faith in human nature. Hold up. He's waffling again.

9:50am. *AAAAAAARGH!...........*I'm going to be late. You know what Trudy's like when you're late? Don't you? Well I do. She gives me that cold look. For someone so pretty, she really can be quite intimidating.

Now something tells me I didn't finish telling you about breakfast. No. Seriously. It's good this bit. Well there I was, minding my own business, tucking into my waffles (which were practically swimming in maple syrup), when this young woman walked by, wearing a tee shirt and sweat pants (tracksuit bottoms). Obviously, I didn't give her a second glance, at first. No. I was far more interested in what lay on the polystyrene plate before me. She passed my table and headed down the corridor towards the swimming pool, only to emerge moments later clad in nothing more than a skimpy bikini. She then strolled (No. Not strolled. She floated.) over to the reception desk, and asked the young guy behind it for a towel. He duly obliged, and she went back to the pool.

'Hey! You haven't been swimming for a long time'. I said to myself. No. Better not. Her boyfriend, or husband, is probably six foot eighteen and broad as a barn door. I did try not to ogle as she walked by, but hell, I'm only human.........oid.........ish. Hey! Haven't I written that once or twice before? Try 73 times. That would be closer to the mark.

It's now 5:50pm, and I've sent Trudy two text messages, however, till now, she has failed to reply to either of them (silly cow). I'm only joking. I *do* care about her. Well, someone's got to. And, can you think of anyone better qualified to worry about people than me? No? Thought not.

I bought twenty stamps, earlier. I can't think why. I positively abhor writing postcards. But wait a minute. Who would complain if I *did* fail to send any cards? Who would dare? And, if anyone did have the audacity to complain, why, I could always say that I was so preoccupied with writing this rubbish, that I just didn't have the time. Now, why do I refer to my writing as rubbish? Well.........I guess I just believe in getting it in before anyone else does. Ah, yes. There certainly *is* method in my madness. Method? Possibly. Madness? Oh, definitely.

6:20pm. Wouldn't you just know it? Is that a question? I'm not too sure. But, I thought I'd play safe and stick a question mark there, just in case. But seriously. Trudy's just sent me a text, saying she's sick as a dog and is going straight home to bed. Poor woman.

Should I go to Farmers for tea?

I panicked a few minutes ago. You see, I was using the computer without it being plugged into the mains and, all of a sudden, the screen went blank. Yes. The battery was flat, or dead, or whatever happens when there is no longer any life in it. Oh, no. All that writing. It's bound to have disappeared (or so I thought). Fortunately, when I plugged it in, the computer reliably informed me that all my work had been saved. Oh, you beautiful machine,

I shall never curse you again. Better not start making promises I can't keep, eh?

Hey! I've just had a thought. Why don't I go to Barts Barbecue for tea? It's only a mile up the road.

Decided to give dinner a miss. Settled instead for an FVC. Well, sometimes you've just got to keep it simple.

Hi there! Me again.

I had another bad night. I went to bed at around 10:15pm, but, once again, I was awake by 1:30am. I just don't understand it, I've never had a problem with sleeping in the past. Never mind. I'm checking out today, and I'm hoping that several hundred miles of driving will sort me out. Yeah. Should get a good night's sleep tonight.

Having said all that, I must have nodded off at about 5:00am, though I awoke again a little after 6:00am.

It's 7:50am, I've just had a light breakfast of Raisin Bran and one cup of coffee. What? Only one? Yes. I know. But it'll keep me going until lunchtime.

I've got half a tank of gas. Should I fill the tank before I go? No. I'll fill it somewhere between here and Knoxville, which is about 250 miles from here. Half a tank will get me over 200 miles.

Now don't even bother asking me where I'm planning on staying this evening, as I have absolutely no idea. In fact, your guess is as good as mine. I'll have a look through my motel guide books when I stop for gas.

6:00pm. Max Meadow, Virginia. Yes. I know. That's just what I thought. What a strange name. Virginia? Sorry. Just being a bit silly. 'So what's new?' I hear you ask. Yes. Very droll. But, what's odd, is that I don't feel in a very silly mood. *Au contraire.* I was, of course, referring to the name of the town: Max Meadow. I have absolutely no idea where the name comes from. One can only *assume* that the town is named after the man who founded it. But then, you know what they say about assumptions? '*When you assume, you make an ASS out of U and ME*'. Oh, please yourself.

Although it hasn't been a bad day, it hasn't been a particularly good one either. Some of it went well, and some of it didn't.

I had hoped to be a lot closer to New Jersey by now, but a guesstimate would put me about 500 miles from there.

I'm not as young as I used to be. When I first started doing road trips, I thought nothing of driving 650 to 700 miles per day. Now, however, I struggle to get through 400 miles, which is approximately what I've done today.

My aim was to get to New Jersey by about 2:00pm tomorrow, check into the motel and spend Saturday afternoon in Manhattan. Now, unless I leave really early tomorrow, there's no way I'm going to make it. What the hell. So long as I can spend the afternoon in New Jersey, that's all that matters.

I left the motel in Dickson at 8:45am. You see? I lost 45 minutes there.

I drove about 180 miles before stopping to fill the tank. I stopped for gas at a service station in the little town of Harriman, Tennessee, which is about 40 miles west of Knoxville. I did say earlier in my report (my report?), that Knoxville was about 250 miles from Nashville. Well, now you know that it is a mere 220 miles.

The tank wasn't empty. In fact, I *probably* would have made it those last 40 miles to Knoxville, but it wasn't worth the risk.

The gas, though not cheap, was far cheaper than some I had purchased on other road trips (In the *Old Days,* you might say). It was $2.39 per gallon, and a tank-full was $26.90.

The trip was pretty uneventful, really. No mistakes on my part. Well, none that I'm owning up to. However, I did forget something. 'What was that?' I hear you ask. Oh, don't be so impatient, *please.*

Last year, I started using a microcassette recorder, for the purpose of recording things like,……… like………erm……… ah, yes. Things like: good songs on the radio, places of interest and thoughts. Yes, thoughts. I do have some interesting ones, you know.

So, there I was, cruising along the highway, wind in my hair, sun on my face, Wait!!!!! What am I talking about? I don't drive a convertible, and I haven't seen the sun, since……since…….. since I last saw it? Oh, talk sense man.

Unfortunately, there were no particular places of interest to give a mention to, however, there were some really groovy sounds coming out of the radio. And so, every time I heard one of those sounds, I simply switched on my trusty device and made a verbal note of it. One small problem. After checking into the motel, I switched on my trusty device, with the intention of jotting down the titles of all those wonderful songs I had recorded (not to mention the names of the artists singing them), but sound came there none. Nope, not so much as a crackle. And why was this? Because, prior to packing my trusty device, I had removed the batteries that had been encased in said trusty device, since this time last year. I had, of course, intended to replace them as soon as I got here, but someone must have forgotten to remind me. Ah, that would be me. *'twas I, said the fly.'*

Never mind. Let's see what I can remember.

Take another little piece of my heart: Janis Joplin.

Imagine: John Lennon (I can feel the tears welling up).

You're so vain: Carly Simon.

Get it on: T Rex.

Free Bird: Lynyrd Skynyrd.

Though there *were* many more, my memory ain't what it used to be.

I'm staying at another Super 8 (which means, I can accumulate a few more Wyndham Rewards Points), though there is nothing super about it. It's more expensive than the one in Dickson ($60.50, as opposed to $52.75), but it's not a patch on it. All I can say in its favour is that I've stayed in worse.

I'll say this, if I say nothing else, 'I've stayed in more motels than you can shake a stick at, and no mistake'. Ah, well. You know what they say: The old ones are the best. Maybe if I say that often enough, I might just start believing it. Yeah. And pigs might........

Dinner.

I dined at the Cookery Restaurant and Buffet.

I've come to a conclusion. So many Americans are not overweight simply because they eat at fast food restaurants as often as they do. No. It's because all of these *so called* fast food restaurants tend to have a set price, all-you-can-eat alternative. Think about it. If I were to tell you that you could eat as much as you wanted for, let's say $5.00, as opposed to $5.00 for one set amount, which option would you choose? This is where the problem lies.

Hey! I'm not just a pretty face. Oh, no. I've got a brain, you know.

If I don't put things down straight away, they are lost forever. Which is why you got my opinion on, all-you-can-eat, before I told you about dinner.

I started with the beef and vegetable soup, which contained something I hadn't eaten in years. Yes. Barley, of all things. To be perfectly honest, I was never that keen on barley when I was a child. Now, however, I find it quite palatable. The soup came with crackers. One simply scrunches the crackers up, and mixes them with the soup. Crackers are also an accompaniment to chilli, which I just adore. Can one *actually* adore a bowl of chilli? Well, I don't know about you, but I give it a bloody good try.

Next, came the meat lover's pasta. Interesting. It was a mixture of spiced meats and sausage, with pasta, in what can only be described as, a beefy, tomato sauce, which was topped with cheese and parsley. This delicacy was accompanied by garlic bread. *'Garlic bread'?* Although I ate it all, I wouldn't order it again. As for my beverage, well that was just a glass of coke. All in all, the meal was average and the bill came to $13.05, plus a $2 tip.

I could really do with an FVC right now, but because of the strange road system they have around here, I fear that if I *were* to venture out in the dark, I wouldn't be able to find my way back until it got light.

8:30pm. Let's see what's on the box. You can't beat a bit of telly.

SATURDAY OCTOBER 17TH

7:00am. I've had breakfast (just Raisin Bran and coffee). While I was in the dining area of the lobby, I got talking to an old guy who *actually* knew where Southport was. Now, there aren't many of *them* around here (Americans who know where Southport is). This guy (when his wife was still alive) had even been to Brighton. Now, why do I say that with such surprise in my voice? A lot of English people go to America for their holidays, while *some* Americans prefer to vacation in England.

Oddly enough, I was discussing words and how they differ between our nations with a lady I got chatting to at breakfast, only yesterday, while I was still in Dickson. To an American, a holiday is just one day: i.e. national holiday. A vacation, on the other hand, is something they take annually.

It's ironic, really. You see, there I was (an Englishman in America), wittering on about how I'd driven over a thousand miles of Route 66, and proudly displaying my Route 66 belt buckle, and then explaining how I intended to drive the entire route (Chicago to Los Angeles) and then the old guy informed me that it was something he had always wanted to do, but sadly, at his age, would now not be able to. I didn't like to ask, but at a guess, I'd say he was in his late seventies, or *even* early eighties. So sad.

I managed around five hours sleep last night, not waking until 3:30am. Yep. Looks like I'll soon be getting a full eight hours. Yeah. That'll be the day before I come home.

7:40am. If I'm to make it to New Jersey by about 4:00pm, then I'll have to be on the road by 8:00am.

But, before I go, just let me say this: "THIS". There. I've said it. So what have you got to say to that? Pretty powerful stuff, I think you'll agree. Some might even say explosive. Who knows? It could even bring down the government.

But seriously. What I wanted to say was that, although I had originally intended to add pictures to this journal, I'm not sure, at this time, whether I really want to, or even could do. Perhaps it's better without the pictures. What do you think? Just let me know, and then I'll file your suggestions under F for important.

Maybe I'll just put several pictures in the middle of…… this……this……whatever it is, and that way, everyone's happy. Problem solved. You'll be wanting blood next.

7:50am. Time I wasn't here.

6:00pm. Now I'm confused. You see, when you travel from Tennessee to New Jersey (which is where I am now), you have to cross one of those time zones. So, why is the clock in my room showing the same time as my watch? Ah! Now then. Wait a minute. It's possible, just ever so slightly possible, that I altered my watch in Virginia, last night. But why don't I remember doing it? I guess it's all this travelling, and not enough sleep. Yeah. That would explain it.

So here I am, in Newark, New Jersey. I'm staying at the Days Hotel, on Highway 1 & 9. And no. Don't even *think* about asking me to explain that. The way I'm feeling right now, I don't even want to write. Do you know how much this hotel is costing me for two nights? It's enough to give you nightmares. 'Yes. This is Mr O'Leary, in room 306, is that room service? Oh, good. Well, could I possibly order a nightmare? And no, you'd better not charge me for it. Well, not if you want to see your next birthday.'

This room (albeit one of the finest, if not *the* finest I've ever stayed in), is costing me $113.95 per night, and I'm booked-in for two nights.

I'm trapped. I'm in a big city, with millions of lanes of traffic and I'm the only driver who has no idea where he is going. Everyone (but everyone), knows exactly what they are doing and where they are going. They shoot onto and off the freeways and interstates, from every direction, at varying speeds. To see it from above, or from the sidelines, must be a wondrous sight. The whole exercise has to be the finest piece of vehicular choreography one could ever imagine. But! Put a novice smack damn in the middle of it, and it's a recipe for disaster. I kid you not.

Oh, how I fucking hate driving in big cities. They are the bane of my life.

Apparently, there is nowhere close where I can get a bite to eat, so it looks like I'll have to eat in the hotel restaurant. God only knows what that's going to cost. Perhaps I should enquire as to whether they have a glass of water, and some dry crackers? Anything else, and I shall end up washing dishes.

But wait! *'I spy with my little eye.'* I've just spotted some freebies. Now what do we have here? A bottle of water, a fruit and nut bar and some *gourmet* popping corn. All I have to do is pop (no pun intended) it into the microwave for a few minutes and, *voila.* ('That's French, by the way.) Well, that's dinner sorted. Just joking. Perhaps I'll eat the freebies when I get back from dinner. Now then, should I put on a clean shirt? What do you think, hm? Oh, sod it. I'll just keep my jacket on. They won't know I've worn the same tee shirt for two days. Two days? Is that all?

Would someone remind me to charge my phone this evening? Good show.

7:00pm. Dinner, I think.

Well, it was as I expected. Bloody expensive.

I knew it was a mistake as soon as I walked in. The place was dimly lit (always a bad sign) and the waiter bowed respectfully every time I opened my mouth to speak (also a bad sign). I studied the menu carefully, though, to be honest, there wasn't an awful lot on it. However, what there was, was grossly overpriced.

I opted for the chargrilled chicken and cheese sandwich, with fries, and the beverage was a coke. Bill? $14.53. Now don't ask me why, but I felt obligated to leave a large tip, so, when the waiter left the bill (in one of those plastic folders they always insist on using), I slipped a $20 bill into it and left before he returned to collect it. Do you realise, that's almost a 38% tip? Silly of me, I know. But. *'What are y' gonna do?'* as they say in these parts.

When I got back to my room, I decided to eat the popcorn. I read the instructions, programmed the microwave and popped the packet into the machine. Hot popcorn. Wonderful. But tell me this. Why is it, that when you reach the bottom of the bag, there are always several kernels that have not popped? Now, under normal circumstances, I would simply have thrown said kernels away, but I was in no mood to waste what was rightfully mine. So, after reprogramming the microwave, I popped the bag in, sat back and waited. But all was not well. Oh no. I noticed a peculiar smell, so I quickly opened the microwave door. Imagine my horror, as a cloud of smoke hit me in the face. Fortunately, the smoke alarm failed to go off. It *could* have been even worse than that. Yes. You see, there are two sprinklers in this room. If they had gone off, I would have been in deep shit. Can you imagine the conversation between me and the hotel management in that event? *'So, Mister O'Leary. Tell me again, and this time with a straight face, just how you managed to set off the sprinkler system in your room.' 'Well……you see……erm……(shouts out loud) It wasn't my fault. The popcorn must have been faulty.'*

There's a label on that bottle of water I told you about, with these few words written on it. It reads: Enjoy this FREE bottle of DASANI. Compliments of Days Inn. Notice how it fails to mention whether the popcorn and the bar of fruit and nut are free, or not. I'll probably get a bill when I check out.

In my room, there are a variety of electrical appliances. One of them just happens to be a coffee maker, complete with regular coffee, decaffeinated coffee and tea. So, what I've decided to do is this: I'll have the fruit and nut bar for breakfast, along with that half bag of mustard flavoured pretzels that I bought in Dickson. I *had* planned to eat them the other night, good job I didn't. And, with the in-room-coffee, very kindly provided by the hotel, I'm sorted. As for dinner, well I'm sure I can find something nice and tasty and *cheap*, while I'm in Manhattan. Yeah. I'll find one of those Subway sandwich shops, and bring a foot-long back to the hotel with me. Once again. Sorted.

I had to gas-up twice today. Once, in Staunton, Virginia and the second time…oh, just across the state line, in West Virginia.

I'm damned if I can remember the name of the place. No matter. It's unimportant.

I still haven't put any batteries in my microcassette recorder. Consequently, I'm having difficulty remembering all the great sounds I heard today. Ah! Wait a second. *Imagine,* by John Lennon was on the radio, as were a couple of Beatles tracks. And, I remembered a great song from yesterday *"Had a bad day"* by Daniel Pouder. I'm not too sure about the spelling of his surname though. Oh! There was *"Do Wah Diddy"* by Manfred Mann.

Unfortunately, I cannot get a bus from the hotel all the way to Manhattan. However, there is a free shuttle bus which will take me from the hotel to Newark Airport, where I can get the Airtrain all the way to New York's Penn Station, located at 33rd Street and 7th Avenue. Money, money, money. For this service, I must pay $15 each way. Oh, how I'll be glad to get out of here. But wait a second. What the hell awaits me in Chicago? More of this? Well, it is a big city. And, you know what I think of big cities. It's unprintable.

11:00pm. Time for bed.

6:50am. Marvellous. Bloody marvellous.

Although this humongous bed is extremely comfortable, and although I did not climb into it until gone 11:00pm, needless to say, I was (once again) awake by 3:30am. I just can't figure out what the hell is going on here. Answers on a postcard, please. No. Scratch that.

It's peeing down outside, which, if it keeps up, means that I won't be going over to Manhattan today. Oh! And the coffee machine is on the blink. But, I must stay positive.

Wait a minute. Wait just one cotton picking minute. I've brought a waterproof coat with me, haven't I? So what's the problem? A little rain never hurt anyone. Hm. I wonder if there are any people out there who are *allergic* to water. Well, it's a medically proven fact that a small proportion of people are, in fact, actually allergic to direct sunlight. I know this to be true, as I once saw a programme on the subject, albeit many years ago. Tragic, really.

Having already polished off the fruit and nut bar, it was time for the pretzels. Have you ever tried mustard flavoured pretzels? You should. They really are quite yummy.

Still raining. I'll put the telly on shortly, and see if there is the *slightest* chance of it brightening up. Did you know, they actually have a weather channel over here?

I had to improvise with the coffee. It's disgusting. Whose idea was it to put coffee in a bag, anyway? Yes, it works with tea, but *not* coffee. Oh no. But, you know me, I need at least one cup per day. Now that I think of it, I *did* only have the one cup yesterday.

I've been trying to think of when I last had a brew as foul as this, or even worse, and I've just remembered. Why! It was only last year, and little more than 20 miles north of here. It was at the Super 8 Motel, in Little Ferry. But, there are pros and cons in every aspect of life. For example: Had I chosen to stay in Little

Ferry once again, it would have cost me little more than $70 per night (as opposed to the $113-95 per night that I'm paying here), the 46 Diner is just two doors away, I'd have but to cross the road to catch the bus into Manhattan and the price for a return ticket would be a mere $6.40 (unless of course, the prices have gone up since last year). Now, beat that. Yes. The Super 8 in Little Ferry *may* leave a lot to be desired, but it does have its advantages.

Now, where the hell did I put those notes? *'Notes, notes, come out, wherever you are.'*

Ah! Now there's a thing. I haven't done so much as one meditation since I got here. Hm. Might just start sleeping better if I got back into it. Meditation, that is.

A week before I came over here, I checked this hotel out on the web. Listen to me. Sounding all professional. Talking like someone who *actually* understands this modern technology. But I digress. I got onto the website and started to fill in the booking application on screen. Obviously, I didn't go ahead with it, but I did give these two nights (Saturday 17th and Sunday 18th), as the dates I would be wanting to stay. The price that was quoted on the site was just $135. Now, I assumed that that price was for the two nights, however, after checking out the price list (which is conveniently pinned to the back of the door, and gives a price of $160 per night), $135 may well have been the cost for just one night. I'll never know now.

My computer is not just for the purpose of keeping a journal. No. I brought it with me, in the vain hope, that by simply being in the same building where they have Internet access, I would be able, not only to access the Internet, but also send and receive emails. How wrong I was. It doesn't work like that. Oh, sure. I *could* use the computers (with their free Internet access), so very kindly provided by all the motels I stay at, in which case, I *would* be able to send and receive emails, but I just don't feel comfortable doing that. Yes. I know. I'm strange. Who knows? Maybe I'll give it a go. But not today.

8:45am. Still raining

Ah! Now then. There's a thing. I told you that this room was full of electrical appliances, didn't I? Well. On the wall, is one of those large, plasma screen TV (televisions, telly, TV. *'You say tomarto, I say tomayto'.* Oh. Some days I despair, I really do.) and, strategically positioned directly below it, is a keyboard, no less. Oh, yes. I *do* have access to the Internet. Unfortunately, the owners of this establishment expect one to pay $9.95 per day, for the privilege of using this facility. *'Not on your nelly.'*

They even have an adult entertainment channel. Now, tempting as it was, it would have cost me a fortune, so, I settled instead for BBC America and an episode of *Keeping up appearances,* followed by an episode of, *As time goes by.* Sad.

I'm still toying with the idea of inserting some photos into this journal. Perhaps I could put photos onto the pages that are only half full. Do you think? We'll see.

Apart from all the appliances (telly, keyboard, fridge, microwave, ironing board, iron, hairdryer (unnecessary) and a very snazzy art deco desk lamp), I even have a safe in my room. Yep. Put all my cash and travellers cheques into it last night. I just shut the door, keyed in a special four digit number and bob's your uncle. The number I keyed in was……Oh, give me a minute. I know this. It was……Oh, shit! *'Excuse me. But, does anyone know a good safe cracker?'*

Should I have my room cleaned, or should I put the "do not disturb" sign on the door? Now, that's what I usually do when I'm only staying for two nights.

Yeah. I'll just put the sign on the door. After all, if they do come in to clean the room *and* leave another bag of popcorn, I might not be so lucky next time. I wouldn't want to burn down the hotel. Oh, no. That would never do.

I'm on the third floor. A sign I read in the lift on the way up, indicated that there were vending machines on the fourth floor. So, if I feel a little peckish, I shall just nip up there and see what's on offer.

I've just had a thought. What if I did pay the $9.95 for Internet access, only to discover that there were no emails for me anyway? I'd be more than a little pissed off about that. No. I'll leave it for now.

I know! I'll just get my umbrella out, and go for a wander around Newark. Newark in the rain, eh? No. Not very tempting.

I feel like Tony Hancock. I'm sat here in my underwear, talking to myself, tapping away on this bloody keyboard and wondering if it's ever going to stop raining. My God. What a life. Is this what I've been reduced to? I could always talk to God, I suppose. But would He be in? And, if He was, would He want to talk to me? When you think about it, that really would be the final nail in the coffin (metaphorically speaking), if even God didn't want to talk to me. But then, he might not work on a Sunday. Well, let's face it, a lot of us take Sunday off, don't we? So, why shouldn't He/She/It? Oh, you get the picture. Still raining out there.

I don't think there's any point in putting the weather channel on, it's grey skies as far as the eye can see.

No. I couldn't possibly enjoy Strawberry Fields on a day like this. And anyway, the musicians are hardly likely to be playing in the rain, are they?

I must get a picture of Trudy when I get back to Dickson. I know! I'll get someone to take one of us both together. That'll brighten up this journal.

I've decided against going to Chicago. No. I'll start my tour of Route 66 just after the Windy City, as it is often referred to. Yes. Somewhere quiet. Out in the open, as it were.

6:45pm. *'I should've stayed home'.*

The rain stopped, and even though it was quite cold, I thought, *'What the hell'*, and headed off to Manhattan.

Easy enough, you might think.

I got the free shuttle service from the hotel to the Airtrain Station, which is basically a monorail that connects Newark International Airport Railway Station with the three air terminals

27

of Newark Airport. From the Airtrain Station, I took the monorail for just one stop to the Railway Station.

The trip from Newark to New York took just 30 minutes, and cost $15. Have I already told you how much it costs? Yes? Oh, what the hell. Now, I don't know whether it has anything to do with my *negativity,* but it seems to me, that my day just isn't complete, unless something goes wrong. All I wanted was the $8.00 ticket, which would have allowed me to make four subway trips. Apparently, one trip is now $2.25 but (obviously) the more you buy, the cheaper it works out. So, I'm at the ticket machine, in the subway beneath Penn Station. I touch the screen in all the right places (as directed), insert a $20 bill and wait for both my ticket, and my change. Of the ticket variety, there was one; of the change variety, there was none. After my ticket was dispensed from the machine, a message appeared on screen, which read: *'Your ticket has been credited with $23'.* There were too many people around for me to start cursing and swearing, but inside I was seething. There was just no way I could spend that amount on the subway in one day. In fact, I would have to stay on here for *at least* another two more days to have any chance of spending what I had left on my card. $18.50, to be precise.

I've just done a few calculations and, I would have to use my subway card another eight times, and I'd *still* be 50 cents in credit.

On the plus side, although I've spent $171.74 today, it's still just under $20 less than my daily budget. Hey! I'm *actually* being positive for a change.

I arrived in New York just after 2:30pm, had a bit of a wander around Strawberry Fields Garden and Central Park and, an hour later, I was on my way back to the station. It wasn't the cold that bothered me, I just felt miserable. I guess, when the weather's bad, New York just isn't a fun place to be.

I don't think I've ever been happier to get back to a motel/hotel.

I put the telly on, put my feet up and tucked into my foot-long sandwich, of turkey, ham, two types of cheese, lettuce, tomato, cucumber, pickle and mustard. Yummy just doesn't cover it. That was only two hours ago, but now I'm hungry again. Hungry or not, I'm not using the hotel retaurant again. I suppose I *could* settle for a bag of pretzels, or a bar of chocolate from the vending machine. But, what would *really* give me a boost right now, is a French Vanilla Coffee. I'd give $10 for one of those. No! Make that $20.

Hey! I've discovered that they actually have free coffee in this place. Unfortunately, it's only served between the hours of 12 midnight, and 6:00am. Now, what the fuck is all that about? Wait a minute. Don't we know someone who's usually awake between those hours? Yes! That would be me.

Who ever heard of a hotel (or motel), being miles away from the nearest eatery? It's no wonder that they can charge so much for their food.

Every time I've been to New York, I've always taken at least one photo of The Dakota, but not today. No. No photo. But, as I walked past it, once again, I fantasized about living there. Ah. One day. Maybe.

Though I didn't take any pictures on this particular trip to Manhattan, I thought I'd add a couple from one of my previous visits. I trust this meets with your approval. Yes?

The Dakota. Where the late, great John Lennon lived.

Strawberry Fields Garden, Central Park.

MONDAY OCTOBER 19^(TH)

8:15am. Well, wouldn't you know it? I said, wouldn't you just flaming well know it? All those days of waking up early, and the one day I *really needed* to be up early (for the free coffee), I manage to have the best night's sleep thus far.

I went to bed at 10:40pm, and didn't wake until 5:30am. Having said that, I still didn't manage to drag myself out of bed until 7:30am.

Yes. At 7:30am, I had a good stretch, climbed out of bed, went straight over to the window, drew back the curtains and what did I see? *'A lot of people staring back at you?'* No! Of course not. I saw that the sun was shining, there was not a cloud in the sky and I? Well, I'm checking out today. Doesn't it just make you want to spit? No! Not on the carpet. Please.

Now, I should head west, towards Route 66, but I'm toying (only toying, mind you) with the idea of heading north, back up to the Super 8 motel that I stayed at last year. You remember the one, don't you? It's in an area of New Jersey called Little Ferry. That way, I'd be able to go back over to Manhattan and use up all that credit I still have on my subway ticket. Oh, come on. It's the principle of it. Isn't it?

Oh, decisions, decisions. What to do, and where to go, and have I got time. I do know one thing for certain. I won't be staying in this establishment ever again. How can one be so close to civilization, and yet be so far away from it? The mind boggles.

Yesterday, I was rummaging (isn't that a great word? *RUMMAGING*. I like it) through my suitcase, and I came across the two batteries that were supposed to be in my microcassette recorder. I vaguely recall taking them out whilst I was packing, thinking at the time, that it would be a good idea to do so. No matter. I shall now be able (with the help of this amazing gadget) to make a note of all those wonderful old (and some new) songs that I keep hearing.

31

Checkout is not until 12 noon. As it's only just 9:00am, I have plenty of time to decide on what course of action to take.

Do I go west, or north?

A coffee would really help me right now. There's some *'DECAF'* on the tray next to the coffee maker, but as the coffee maker isn't working, I'd have to improvise and cook the coffee bag in the microwave (with some water, of course), which *might not* be such a good idea. Having said that, I did boil some water in the microwave only yesterday, so I could have a cup of tea.

I'm such a fool. If only I'd let them clean my room yesterday, they might have put some more freebies in here. Damn.

There were two complimentary mints on the desk when I arrived. Sadly, both are long gone. I suppose, I *could* eat one of those bags of sugar. No. Now I'm just being silly.

Eureka! The vending machines. Of course. Why didn't I think of them sooner?

Pretzels and a candy bar, I think. It's just a shame they don't do coffee in those machines.

Result.

I got my supplies from the vending machine (a Nutri-Grain bar, a bag of potato skins, (crisps) a bag of mini pretzels and a bag of Granola), and while I was there, I found 36 cents on the floor. Now wasn't that lucky? I ate the potato skins in about 20 seconds, then moved onto the Granola. But what is Granola? I would describe it as being similar to Honey Nut Clusters. Obviously, it should be served in a bowl, with milk. But, as I had neither bowl, nor milk, I ate it as was. Hell! I was so hungry, it was all I could do to stop myself from eating the wrapper.

Now then. Pretzels, or Nutri-Grain Bar? Hm. Tricky.

5:30pm. No. It's not the *actual* writing that bugs me anymore. Oh, crumbs no. Although my typing skills are limited (that's putting it mildly. I still favour the one finger method), I have to admit, I *do* quite enjoy it. But why, oh why, must I have to scroll through every damn page, before reaching the part where I last left off? What did you say this was? *Modern technology?* I never had this problem with pen and paper, you know. Of course, when I get home, some smart arse will say, '*Oh! Didn't you know? All you have to do is press ABC, XYZ, and you go straight to your last page.*' Or something like that.

As to my location at this present moment in time, I'm staying at a particularly fine establishment, in Clearfield, Pennsylvania. And yes. It's one of my old favourites, a Super 8 Motel. And not only that, there's an absolutely gorgeous, blonde lady at reception. I wonder if I could *wow* her with tales of my travels? Maybe.

I'm hungry. I haven't eaten since.........since..........since the last time I ate. Well, I have difficulty remembering, sometimes. You know the score.

Right! I'm off to the Dutch Pantry for dinner.

7:20pm. Oh, yes. Oh, yes yes yes yes yes.

Well, there's another eatery to add to the, '*O'Leary's Good Food Guide*'.

I would find it extremely difficult (if not impossible), to give *any* restaurant 10/10.

In fact, *any* restaurant would have to be pretty damn special to get a 9/10. And so, although the Dutch Pantry cannot be given either of these marks, it is certainly worthy of an 8/10. Three cheers for the Dutch Pantry.

I started with a salad (well, let's face it, I haven't had much in the way of salads and vegetables since I arrived, so this was healthy food), of lettuce, tomato, onion, cheese, croutons and (of all things) raw broccoli, which wasn't that bad with the Italian dressing. This was followed by the Shrimp Skewers. Two skewers, with five shrimps on each, accompanied by a spicy tomato sauce. I bet your mouth's watering, isn't it? Then, I plumped for Veal Parmesan. (Is that spelt correctly? It doesn't look right to me.) A slice of veal in breadcrumbs, on a bed of spaghetti, topped with spicy tomato sauce and cheese and two doorstops of Texas toast, with which to mop-up all that delicious sauce. Along with a glass of Pepsi, and a mug of coffee, the whole meal came to a mere

$18.83. The waitress (whose name eludes me at this time, though I'm sure I'll remember it later), received a $3 tip.

So, if ever you should find yourself out this way, just pop in and tell them Brendan sent you. No. Don't do that. They won't have the foggiest idea what (or even who) you're talking about.

'I'm famous'. But only inside my own head.

Dessert. Unfortunately, I was *"fit-to-busting"* as they say, so I had to give dessert a miss. However, I was amazed to see some of the delights they had on their menu. Apart from the usual suspects: Strawberry Shortcake, Hot Fudge Cake, New York Style Cheese Cake and a variety of Meringue and Fruit Pies, they *actually* had, wait for it, wait for it: Bread and Butter Pudding, topped with cinnamon sauce and whipped cream, Apple Dumpling (again, topped with cinnamon sauce) and finally, Rice Pudding, with sweet, plump raisins. Admit it. You're slavering again, aren't you? Yes. I thought you would be.

Now, those three desserts are not what one would expect to find on a menu in *this* country. England, yes. But not here. If only I were here for three more days, then I could sample them all. Ah, well. Maybe next year?

Getting out of New Jersey was easier than I thought it would be. I had visions of myself going round in circles for hours and hours, like some demented goldfish. Fortunately, the gods were on my side. Or, was there a guardian angel who just happened to be going to Pennsylvania? Your guess is as good as mine.

After leaving Newark, I stopped for gas in a little town called Clinton, which is only about 50 miles west of Newark, and just off Interstate 78, at exit 15. I filled up at a Pilot service station, where the gas was just $2.33 per gallon. The tank was close to empty, so took $26 worth of fuel.

While I was there, I got my *fix* of coffee (an FVC) and an apple danish. Although slightly chilly, with a gentle breeze, the sun was high enough to provide sufficient warmth, so I sat at one of the picnic tables, ate my danish, drank my coffee and pondered life, the universe and all that shit. *'What the fuck is it all about?*

And what is it all for?' I wondered to myself. It's such a crying shame that I couldn't come up with any answers. But, you know what they say: *'There are more questions than answers.'*

Interstate 78 goes deep into Pennsylvania, before being taken over by Interstate 81, about 15 miles north east of Harrisburg, which, incidently, is the capital of Pennsylvania. (Geography lessons, too. Is there nothing this boy can't do?) When I reached Harrisburg, I headed north on Highway 11/15, which splits just north of Sunbury, where Highway 11 goes north east and Highway 15 continues north, towards Interstate 80, which was where I started heading west again.

I made only one other stop (at a rest area off exit 192, which is about 70 miles east of where I am now). This was simply to refer to my motel guide books, and decide upon a suitable place in which to put my head down for the night.

By the way. The gorgeous blonde lady at reception is called Robin. Oh, I do hope I dream about her tonight. Such a beautiful lady. Do you suppose that one day I may just be lucky enough to settle down with a lady like her? What am I asking you for? You neither know, nor care. *'I talk to the trees, that's why they put me away'.* Steadily moving on.

Big city drivers are impatient, always in a rush and have absolutely no sympathy or compassion for the interloper, or humble tourist who has the *audacity* to stray into their territory. Yes. The big city driver is a rare breed. A seasoned professional, skilled in the art of driving under the most difficult of conditions and does not suffer fools gladly. If I spent enough time driving in one of those areas, would I become just like them? Uncaring? Unfeeling? Devoid of any emotion? Fuck it! I don't want to be a big city driver.

Music. This is what you've all been waiting for, isn't it?

Lyin' Eyes: The Eagles. This song takes me back to The British Wye, a ship I was on in 1976. I joined that ship on March 24th, in a place called Bandar Mahshahr, Iran. After spending one night in the Abadan International Hotel, myself and two other crew members took the hour and a half taxi ride to the ship. However, on arriving at the refinery, which we had to travel through before boarding our vessel, we encountered a big problem, or at least, I did. You see, I had no passport, and the security guards were not prepared to let me enter the facility without one. Fortunately for me, the shipping agent managed to talk them round, and I was able to join my ship. Shame, really. I was looking forward to going back home. Bandar Mahshahr is as far as the ships travel up the Shatt Al-Arab Waterway. But that's quite enough of that. We'll talk about it another time, okay?

Smoke On The Water: Deep Purple. This one takes me back even further. It always reminds me of Maria's Bar, in Skaramanga, Greece, and The British Commerce, in 1975. Ah! Now that was September 16th, and my second trip to sea. It was a pretty good trip……what I can remember of it. Yes yes yes. Alright. So I was pissed, most of the time. I was young and foolish, and I was just out for a good time. It's not a crime, is it? Greece, Italy, Turkey, Syria, Nigeria and God knows where else. I'm damned if I can remember. God, I feel old.

The Heart Goes On: Celine Dion. This song reminds me of Irene May. One of, if not, *The* greatest woman I've ever had the privilege of knowing. It's been ten years since she died, but she'll always be in my heart. One very special lady. Irene was married to Fred (one of the nicest guys I ever met, a real gent), and between 1979 and 1984, they ran a pub called The Hoghton Arm, in Southport. Oh, what fun. Such happy times. Though the times are gone, the memories live on.

Oh, What A Night: Frankie Valli and The Four Seasons. Great song.

That Don't Impress Me Much: Shania Twain. Did I ever tell you that her real name is, Eileen Edwards? Well it is. So there.

I also heard two good songs while I was eating dinner.

There She Goes: Originally, by The La's, though this particular version was being sung by a female artist, whose name I know not.

Crazy For You: Probably. No. Definitely Madonna's finest song. Come to think of it, it's the only one of her songs that I *really* like.

10:20pm. Have I been at this for three hours?

It's at times like this that I wish I was still using pen and paper. I would have been finished two hours ago. I hope you people appreciate all this effort.

Super 8 Motel. Clearfield, Pennsylvania.

Dutch Pantry. Clearfield, Pennsylvania. You'll not regret eating here.

8:45am. Though this is a beautiful room, in an equally beautiful motel, and though the bed was comfortable enough, I slept very badly. This was due (in no small part) to the infernal noise made by the refrigerators (that's what they call them over here. But why do we—the British—abbreviate it to fridge? There isn't even a D in Refrigerator. Curious.) they insist on installing in every room. My own (as per usual), I unplugged before retiring to bed. However, I was constantly woken by the sound of those *totally unnecessary* devices in the adjacent rooms.

Yesterday, whilst at the visitors centre where I stopped to check my motel guide books, I purchased a small bag of Honey, Mustard and Onion flavoured Pretzel Pieces. As I chomped my way through that little delicacy, I pondered on the mystery of how the hell such a product could be made, and whose conception it was. Although I had no idea as to the identity of the creator (and probably never would), I did, however, come up with a method of producing such a delectable snack. It is as follows: First. Take a whole, stale pretzel and break it into smallish pieces. Then, immerse these pieces in a marinade of honey, mustard and onion. (The onion would, more than likely, be minced up.) Finally, after draining off the excess marinade, one would simply deep-fry (or shallow-fry) the pieces. *Et voila!* (There's that French again.) The consistency of this little delicacy is similar to that of a Crunchie bar (for those of you who know what one is, of course), though much harder.

Crunchie bars, eh? When was the last time I ate one of those?

Nostalgia.

What is the definition of nostalgia? For me, it is the belief that although I *appear* to be travelling in one particular direction, in reality, I am doing the complete opposite. Deep, man. You know, the more I read that, the less sense it makes. Ah, well. Never mind. Nostalgia isn't what it used to be.

Yes. I have one foot in the present and one foot in the past, but I'm afraid to take a step forward in case I lose touch with everything I know and understand.

Now, I know that I've written the following several times before, but Lennon does put it so beautifully. Take it away, John.

'How can I go forward when I don't know which way I'm facing? How can I explain something I'm not sure of?'

Those lines come from a song called: *How*, written in 1971, if I remember rightly.

Though I brought two books with me, I did very little reading on the plane, and absolutely none at all since I arrived.

Even if I were not writing this journal, I would (more than likely) be spending most of my evenings in front of the box, rather than have my nose in a book, even if one of those books is by Stephen Fry. Although I am a fan of Stephen Fry, given a choice between reading one of his great works and telly......Sorry Stephen, but telly wins every time.

A journal should not be *just* a record of one's travels. No. It should also inform the reader about the character of the writer himself, even if the reader *is* the writer. Perhaps this should come under the heading of, *Self Analysis*. Yes?

Oh, come on. This is the real world. It's not all sweetness and light.

Or, to put it another way, *'If you can't take the heat, get out of the fucking kitchen'*.

It's just after 10:00am. Time I made a move. Don't think I'll make it to Route 66 by this evening, but that's okay.

8:10pm. Oh, what a day.

I've just got back from having dinner in (of all places) a bar. Yes! I did say *BAR*. I *shall* go into detail at some point, just don't expect it to be today.

Oh, what the hell. There probably isn't anything worth watching on the box, so I might as well keep writing.

But first. For the past few days, every time I've switched the computer on, it tells me that my Norton Anti-Virus has expired (or words to that effect), consequently, I'm not fully protected. But how can that be? I haven't had it a year yet. Anyway, there's nothing I can do about it here. I'll get it sorted out when I get home.

I put gas in the car four times today. On three occasions I just put $5 worth in, and on the other, I put $10 worth in. You see, after I crossed the state line, from Pennsylvania into Ohio, the price of gas shot up. (By that, I mean it was more expensive.) But I (misguidedly as it happens) believed that if I only put small amounts of gas in my car at all these expensive gas stations that I kept coming across, I would, eventually, find an inexpensive one. Not so. Maybe I'll have better luck when I cross into Indiana in the morning.

When I left Clearfield, this morning, I had absolutely no idea as to where I would be spending the night. I figured I'd just head in a westerly direction, and stop when I felt like it.

I was heading west, the sun was going down (making driving a little awkward), and as I was getting a little tired, I decided to start heading south, on Interstate 75. It was nothing more than a ten minute drive down to Lima. There's no shortage of motels in Lima, but at every one, when I asked for a room, I got the same reply, *'Sorry. We're all booked up.'* And the reason for this? Apparently, they're having problems with a refinery around here. Which meant they had to contract several hundred workers in, or something like that. All I know, is that there was no room at the inn for little old me.

I got chatting to the guy at reception at the Howard Johnson Motel, and he suggested I try the Microtel in Delphos, which is where I am now. It's about a 30 mile drive from Lima, so I managed to get here before dark. I do so hate driving in the dark. Don't you?

This is a brand new motel, and there aren't any smoking rooms in it. Even when one is in a non-smoking room, if there

41

is a smoking room next to it, one can always smell the cigarette smoke.

When I say new, I couldn't tell you when it opened exactly, but it does have that new smell. In fact, when I walked into my room (which, incidentally, though small, is beautifully furnished), I got that smell of a new baby. Does that sound strange? So, what if it does? That's just what it was like. Anyway. You know what I mean. Babies *do* have that clean, fresh smell to them, don't they?

All the motels in Lima (even the ones that are normally expensive) had signs outside, giving the prices of the rooms. And get this. The prices ranged from as little as $33 minimum, up to a maximum of $39. Strange. And what am I paying? $71.99. Just don't annoy me. I'm having a bad day.

9:15pm. I don't want to write anymore. I'll fill you in on the rest of the day's events in the morning.

8:25am. Yep. It's official. I'm getting up later and later as the holiday progresses.

I finally managed to crawl out of bed just before 7:30am, having had yet another restless night. And the cause of my restlessness? The bed was too damn soft. Now, explain to me (if you can), how it is possible for a person to be unable to sleep because they are *too* comfortable? It defies logic.

I climbed onto this very large bed (a bed so high off the ground, that I even considered phoning reception and asking if I could borrow a stepladder), and sank into its soft, warm mattress. It enveloped me. It held me tight, like being in the arms of a loved one. And yet, I could not sleep. Well, not for several hours, anyway. But at some point, I must have dozed off and, I *do* remember dreaming. Brian May was in one of my dreams. I remember having a long chat with him about the difficulties of performing live on stage. I was tempted to bring up the subject of Freddie Mercury, and his untimely death, but thought better of it. After all, they weren't just band members, they would have been close friends too. So, I considered the subject too personal.

Dreams. What was the significance of that dream? Anyone know?

As I have already said, I arrived later than I would have liked last night. This meant that I didn't get to eat until late. Eating late. Not a good idea. However, I had had nothing since breakfast, and was in need of some sustenance, so I headed off in search of a diner, restaurant, café, greasy spoon, *anything*.

On Second Street, two doors from the local police station, I happened upon the Rustic Café. It was an insignificant looking place, though strangely inviting. Something about it seemed familiar. But what? There were neon signs in the window, though apart from noticing the colours (green, red and blue), I paid them little attention.

I opened the door, took but one step inside and then it hit me. Yes. The *smell* hit me. This wasn't just a café. No. This was, wait for it......wait for it......*A BAR*. Oh, no. Several patrons turned and stared at me, as if expecting to see an old regular. I desperately wanted to turn around and beat a hasty retreat, but something wouldn't let me. I felt compelled to enter, with the intention of having nothing more than a bite to eat.

The beautiful neon signs, of green and red and blue, were advertising *Miller Lite* and *Budweiser*, and I could hear them shouting, *'DRINK ME!, DRINK ME!'*.

So many memories came flooding back. Good times *and* bad times.

I strolled over to the bar and spoke to a woman who was sitting on a bar stool, but looked as if she worked there. *"Do you serve food?"* I asked. *" Yes we do."* She replied. *"Would you like a menu?"* She asked. *"Yes. Thank you."* I replied, and walked towards one of the many small booths. The booths were basic. Simple wooden seats and tables. Not particularly comfortable, but then this was a bar not some high class restaurant.

I studied the menu carefully, though it was far from extensive. Simple fare, but, as it turned out, good nonetheless.

I surveyed my surroundings, like an undercover agent on a mission. On the wall behind the bar were two large television sets. One was on the weather channel while the other was on, what appeared to be a programme about construction (or was it destruction?).

Two booths from where I sat there was an old guy drinking coffee while staring at the second screen, as if somehow trapped by its hypnotic power. And that was with the sound turned off.

The room itself was long and narrow, as if not originally designed to be a bar. No. I suspected that it was a converted store, that had long since gone out of business. Delphos is a small town. And, as we all know by now, small towns, with their small populations, sometimes find it difficult to survive.

At the back of the bar was a pool table, where four guys noisily competed against one another.

From time to time, one of the guys would walk over to the juke box (which was situated close to the door), and put a few more songs on.

Was it Creedence Clearwater Revival who sang, *Have you ever seen the rain?* I don't know. But, yes thanks. I have seen the rain. All the fucking way from Tennessee, right up to New Jersey, and then some.

I'm just waiting on a lady: The Rolling Stones.

Yeah. I know what you mean.

About six booths down from me sat a young couple, who laughed and joked, though I didn't catch any of their conversation. At the bar sat two guys, who drank beer, chatted and occasionally stared at the mute, second television.

A young woman (in her early thirties, I guess) walked into the bar on her own, and sat down just two stools away from one of the guys. She had fair hair, wore jeans, a tee shirt and a zip-up sweat shirt. She ordered a beer and then some food, though I couldn't see what she ate. The guy closest started up a conversation with her. Did they know each other, or was he trying to chat her up? I had no idea.

There were shelves on the walls, with a variety of *tacky* trophies on them. You know the ones I mean. They look like they are made of silver, or gold, but are mostly just plastic, with silver and gold paint on them.

Two women worked behind the bar. One served the drinks, while the other prepared the meals. It was a strange set-up. The food preparation area, with its grill and fryer, was behind the bar, adjacent to the beer pumps and optics. One would normally expect to find the food being prepared in a separate room. But it didn't bother me.

I ordered the chicken tenders (three pieces of chicken breast, coated in breadcrumbs and fried), along with hash browns (which were mixed with onions and topped with melted cheese) and a side

order of breaded, fried mushrooms. With my meal I had several
beers and, after paying the bill, I left the bar feeling ever so slightly
intoxicated, yet happy. All in all, it was a pretty good evening.
But how would I get back to my motel? After all, I'd never driven
whilst under the influence of alcohol, and the police station was
only spitting distance away. Damn. What the fuck was I going
to do? *'Yeah. That's it.'* I said to myself. *'I'll walk back to my motel,
and then come and pick up the car in the morning. Hey! It's only
two miles.'* I'M JOKING! Do you think I'm that fucking stupid?
I haven't had a drink in over 23 years, and I'll be damned if I'm
going to ruin it all now.

Now, don't lie to me. I know *exactly* what you were thinking.
You thought I'd weakened and had a drink, didn't you? *Oh, ye of
little faith.* How could you? I'm very disappointed in you.

The bill came to just over $11 (can't remember how many
cents it was), so I left $15. Oh! I nearly forgot. I had two glasses
of coke, and the chicken came with barbecue sauce.

As I was paying the bill, the woman I first spoke to, asked if
I was German. *"No. I'm English."* I replied. *"Well, now you know
where we are, come back and see us sometime."* She said. *"Yes. I might
just do that."* Was my reply. Will I ever return? Who knows?

10:45am. Check-out's not until 12 noon, so I've got plenty
of time.

This room has one of those 32 inch plasma screen televisions
on the wall. Very nice. Come to think of it, the hotel in New
Jersey had one too. Or did I already tell you that? Well, I'm so
sorry for repeating myself. I *do* hope that it hasn't spoiled your
entertainment. Heaven preserve us. We wouldn't want that, now
would we? There's just no pleasing some people.

Music.

Maggie May: Rod Stewart

I wanna know what love is: Originally by Foreigner, though
this version was sung by Mariah Carey.

Had a bad day. Daniel Pouder: (Think I've spelt his name
right.)

Everything I do: Brian Adams.

Band of gold: Freda Payne. (Fantastic song.)

Nowhere Man: The Beatles.

Sweet home Alabama: Lynyrd Skynyrd.

I hope you dance: Lee Ann Womack. (Simply amazing.)

Lola: The Kinks. (Great song.)

You've got a friend: James Taylor.

Build me up buttercup: The Foundations. (I actually bought this single when it first came out. When was that? I remember selling it to my elder brother several years later, for 30 pence.)

Reason to believe: Rod Stewart.

Go your own way: Fleetwood Mac.

Happy to be stuck with you: Huey Lewis and The News.

11:10am. That's about it for now folks. If I've forgotten anything, I'll include it in this evening's update.

5:10pm. Well, it's been different, I'll say that.

Driving can be much more fun when one gets away from the interstates and major highways. Admittedly, if one is not vigilant (especially when driving through small towns, where the signs are not always so clear), one can easily miss a right or left turning. I speak from experience folks, so be told.

At present, I am in the town of Remington, Indiana, and a mere 20 miles from the Illinois state line. Come on. Admit it. You have absolutely no idea what I'm talking about, do you? Never mind. Just nod your head from time to time, and make like you understand. Okay?

Before leaving Delphos (at 11:45am) I had breakfast and then put $20 worth of gas in the tank, just to be on the safe side.

However breakfast wasn't the usual affair. Oh no. Apart from my usual Raisin Bran, I had a banana, as it occurred to me that I wasn't eating enough fruit. This was followed by, what can only be described as, a brown bread raisin filled bagel, which I toasted and had with butter and cream cheese. It was different, I'll give you that. And, with two cups of coffee inside me, I was ready to face anything that life could throw at me. Well, almost.

After putting that $20 worth of gas in the tank, I thought it wise to clean the windshield, which, after all the driving I'd done, was caked with bugs. Yes. I know that I moan when it rains, but at least the windshield stays clean. After a few days on the road, my windshield looks as though I've been caught in the crossfire of a paintball fight.

After leaving Delphos, I stayed with Highway 30, until I reached the little town of Van Wert (15 miles west of Delphos), where I had a little drive around. I stopped there for a while, just to decide upon a suitable route across Indiana. I opted for a more scenic route, which turned out to be the 224. Unfortunately, when I reached the town of Huntington, Indiana, I took a wrong turn and drove several miles north, on the 5. Silly me. Remember what I told you about small towns?

Of course, the mistake I made was in not studying the map properly. You see, in Huntington, the 224 terminates, and you have to take the 24 to keep heading west. And this wasn't the only mistake I made. No. About 50 miles west of Huntington, in the town of Logansport, I missed my turning and drove about 10 miles north on the 35 before realizing my mistake. Now you may be wondering why I don't put the word Highway before these numbers. 'Why does he keep referring to them as, *the 24* and, *the 35*?' Simple. You see, some of these smaller roads are classed as *state routes*, or *county roads* and, as I'm not sure which is which, you'll just have to settle for *"the"*. Boy. Am I glad we got that cleared up.

Yes. I know you'd appreciate it if I kept going, but it's 6:15pm and I haven't eaten since breakfast, so you'll just have to wait. Read a book. Go for a walk. Phone a friend. I'll get back as soon as I can.

Dinner in the Iron Skillet, I think.

7:40pm. I'm back. And I'm not alone. *I wish.*

But seriously. After leaving the Iron Skillet (more of that in a minute), I went into the store next door and purchased a 20 ounce cup of FVC, and this for a mere $1.27. That's less than one English pound. Considerably less, in fact.

'So what did you eat? And what was it like?' I hear you ask. (As though you care.) Well, if you'd really like to know, let's just say, it looked far better on the menu than it did on the plate.

I ordered the *Captain's Seafood Platter*. Though, apart from the deep fried prawns (they call them shrimps in America), I had absolutely no idea what the other two varieties of fish were. The meal came with fries, tartare sauce and spicy tomato sauce, all washed down with a glass of Pepsi.

So, where were we up to, before I so *inconsiderately* left you to go to dinner?

Before we go on, I have a question. Yes. I know full well that you don't like answering questions, but I make the rules here, and if you don't like it, then fuck off.

Question: Why do I find blonde women so appealing? Not that I discriminate against redheads, brunettes, or even women with black hair, for that matter. Some people say that, *'gentlemen prefer blondes'*. Hogwash! You wouldn't describe me as a gentleman, would you? Alright. You didn't *have* to agree with me on that point.

Man, that coffee's good.

A Dodge Neon overtook me this afternoon. And it was in that very make and model that I was stopped and fined for speeding back in 2000 (which was, as you know, the year of my first road trip). Okay. I'll come clean. In truth, I was stopped and fined twice in the space of two days. Once in Tennessee, which cost me $174, and the second time was in Virginia, which cost me $75. So remember kids, speeding is not only dangerous, it's also fucking expensive.

Hey! Did you know that they have a Dan Quayle Museum in Huntington? I didn't go there, but, but, but......but at least I saw the sign. Dan Quayle? Whatever happened to him? Now don't quote me on this, but if I'm not mistaken, I think he was vice president to George Bush senior. Do you suppose he's still in politics?

Now, if memory serves, I'm pretty sure that I was still driving through Huntington, when I saw a sign in the distance, which showed gas at $2.06 per gallon. *YIPPEE!* However, as I pulled up to it, I was disappointed (though not surprised) to see that the gas station had shut down. The gas around these parts is anything from $2.65, to $2.69. Far more expensive than back home in Tennessee. *'Back home in Tennessee?'* Yeah. You got a problem with that? To be perfectly honest, I feel more at home there, than I do in Southport. Sad. But true. *'Home is wherever I feel happy.'*

Music. This is the part you've all been waiting anxiously for.

Cupid. And. *You send me*: Sam Cooke. Now when was the last time you heard either of those songs?

Layla: Eric Clapton. He formed a band called Derek and the Dominos. That was back in 1973, if memory serves.

Leavin' on a jet plane: was that Peter, Paul and Mary? It all depends on my mood. Sometimes that song makes me really happy and then, at other times, it makes me really sad.

Daniel: Elton John.

Would I lie to you?: The Eurythmics.

Is this love?: White Snake.

Cruel to be kind: Nick Lowe. This is one of my favourite songs. If you don't know it, then just listen to it on YouTube. It's fantastic.

Angel of the morning: not sure *who* sang this one, but it's a bloody good song.

I'm a believer: The Monkees. I like The Monkees.

Hold my hand: Hootie and the Blowfish. I can't explain it, but it just has a certain sound. You know what I mean.

The way you love me: Faith Hill. It's a wonderful song, but, *This Kiss* is even better.

Pretty Woman: by the inimitable Roy Orbison.

Build me up buttercup: The Foundations. We had this the other day, but did you know that it was on the soundtrack of the movie, 'There's something about Mary'?

And finally. Can I have a fanfare of trumpets, please?

Baba O'Reilly: THE WHO. Possibly, the greatest band of all time. I get one hell of a buzz every time I hear this song. Those of you who are familiar with the song, will, I'm sure, understand exactly what I mean. And for those of you who love crime dramas, as I myself do, this is the theme tune to CSI New York.

It's 9:00pm, the coffee's all gone and I think we've covered just about everything. So, it's goodnight from me, and it's goodnight from him. We're a double act, don't you know.

THURSDAY OCTOBER 22ND

9:00am. Not much to say this morning. However, I'm sure I can come up with some rubbish or other.

I had a really bad night. Perhaps it was all down to that 20 ounces of FVC. (Have you noticed that, F,V and C form a neat little triangle on the keyboard?)

I went to bed just after 11:00pm, but I was awake before 2:00am. Sadly, I was *still awake* at 6:00am, though shortly after that I must have dozed off for a while, and then forced myself to get out of bed just after 7:30am. I didn't want to get up, but I had to shower and shave, have breakfast (cornflakes, two slices of toast with strawberry jam and two cups of coffee) and write my journal, and all before 11:00am. Yep. They chuck you out of this place at 11:00am. It was 12 noon at my last motel.

I'm in room 125, at the back of the motel, right next to the stairwell. Now there's a word we'd never use in England. *Stairwell.* Interesting. We just call them stairs. But wait a minute. Do stairs become *stairwell*, when situated in a certain part of a building? Maybe they do. No! No! No! *Stairwell* isn't the same as stairs......idiot.

There are a lot of truckers staying here, though that's not surprising, as Remington is just a stone's throw from Interstate 65.

I'm staying at another Super 8, though I'm not at all happy with what I am paying, $82.34. Yes. That's just for one night. Outrageous. Still. There's only one other motel around here (Sunset Inn), and I didn't like the look of that place. Yes. No doubt it was cheaper, but they probably don't provide a free breakfast, and they are not on the Wyndham Rewards Points List. Fortunately, the last place I stayed at (Microtel) has become a recent addition to the list. Lucky old me.

Some of those truckers make one hell of a racket when using the stairs. It's akin to a herd of elephants on the rampage. Of course, it would not be wise to bring this fact to their attention, as some of those guys make Giant Haystacks look like slimmer of the year. BIG, MAN.

I can't understand why every time I put on a clean tee shirt, it smells musty. Not dirty, you understand, just musty. I mean. Several hour before I did my packing, I sprayed the inside of my suitcase with Febreze. Not to worry. It's not like anyone ever gets close enough to notice.

On the subject of dirty tee shirts, it's about time I did some laundry. Looks like I'll be staying for two nights in the next town, wherever that may be. Somewhere in Illinois, I guess, and on Route 66, I should imagine. About time too. I should have been there days ago. But you see, that's the beauty of road trips. You don't actually have to be anywhere, at any given time. Just go with the flow. Go wherever the road takes you, man.

Yeah. You can keep your beaches, and your Benidorm, with its sun, sand and Sangria. *And* its lunatic yobs, who just want to get pissed-up, start fights and then brag about how they got arrested and had to spend a night in the cells. Oh, sure. If that's what they want, then let them get on with it. All *I'm* saying is this. It's not a holiday. Not in my eyes. But then, what do I know? Some people (and they may be right) think I'm a lunatic. Yeah. Like I give a flying fuck.

It's what they call fall, over here. That's autumn, to you.

One might even say, that Mother Nature is casting off her light, flimsy summer attire, in favour of her more sturdy autumn wear. At this time of year, out in the countryside, the scenery is perfectly spectacular.

By the time I reach the next town (Goodland), which is approximately 8 miles down the road, and still in Indiana, it will be an hour earlier than it is here, and that's because I shall be crossing one of those time zones. Travelling west, you gain time. Travelling east, you lose it. *Swings and Roundabouts.*

10:10am. Time to get packed up. Catch you later.

5:15pm. Well that was fun. Not.

I left Remington, Indiana at 11:00am and 8 minutes later it was 10:08am. We've already covered time zones, haven't we? Well, you should have been paying attention then, shouldn't you? I'm not going over all that again, you'll just have to ask another member of the class. Just promise me you'll buck up. Oh, I do despair, some days.

About 15 miles west of Remington, in the town of Kentland, I headed north on Highway 41, before linking up with my old friend, Highway 30, which I took for the 50 or so miles all the way to the town of Joliet, which is south west of Chicago. Perhaps, one day, I may just be brave enough to negotiate my way through the busy sections of Chicago's Route 66. Sadly, it won't be on this trip.

I am, at present, ensconced in a Super 8 motel, in the tiny town of Chenoa, which in case you were wondering is approximately 20 miles north east of the town of Normal, Illinois. Now, although originally I *had* planned to stay in the interestingly named town of Normal, as most people I know would describe me as anything but normal, I decided that I didn't really have any right to. Agree. Disagree. Makes no difference to me.

I really would have loved to spend a little time in Joliet (it's quaint and compact, in fact, perfect for a sightseer on foot), however, just as I arrived, so did the rain. As I was loath to get my *beautiful* leather jacket wet, I decided (like Chicago) that it would keep for another trip. *'Doh!'*, said Homer Simpson.

I *did* make a few mistakes in Joliet (driving down the same streets more than once. Well, it's damn difficult to drive and check one's guide book at the same time), though nothing serious.

Please! Please! Please! Promise me you'll never drive and read a guide book at the same time. I know I shouldn't, but I'm stupid. Of course, this is why normal people never travel alone. *'A co-pilot, a co-pilot, my kingdom for a co-pilot.'* Bah! Humbug!

Shortly after leaving Remington, a grey squirrel ran across the road in front of me. Though I didn't hit it, when I looked in my rear view mirror, the little bugger ran straight back again.

Question: Why did the squirrel cross the road?

Answer: I have no idea. But, as he obviously didn't like it over there, he went straight back.

Oh, come on. You weren't expecting a joke, were you?

6:10pm. Time for dinner.

Chenoa Family Retaurant. Definitely an 8/10. The place itself was stylish (though not overly so), the staff were really friendly (without being patronizing) and the food was excellent. I started with the creamy potato soup, followed by the 14 ounce New York steak, which came with mashed potato (smothered in a rich gravy), green beans, onion rings and a bread roll, all washed down with two glasses of Pepsi. The price? A mere $16.66. That's about a tenner back home. Now you can't grumble at that, can you? Oh! And I left a $3 tip for the waitress.

After the merriment in Joliet, I soon found myself experiencing similar problems in the town of Pontiac. It was like being on a bloody merry-go-round. I just kept going round and round.

Hey! Haven't I driven two of them there Pontiacs? Yeah, man. Beautiful cars.

From Joliet, all the way down to Lexington (a distance of about 85 miles), Route 66 is in places, covered over by Highway 35. This means that one's journey is spent alternating between the two, which can be a little tricky at times. *'None but the brave.'*

Initially, I was (as you would imagine) excited to transfer, once again, from Highway 35 to another section of the old road. It all started well enough. I kept my eyes peeled for the Route 66 markers, positioned conveniently by the sides of the road. I did not deviate. I followed the route carefully, always travelling in the direction of the pointing arrow, but I kept going round in circles. *'Wait a minute. Haven't I already been down this road once, twice, three times?'* I found myself saying. Pontiac. A lovely town, I'm sure. But how the fuck was I to get out of here? It was as though the town was refusing to let me go. In the end, I decided to ignore one of the arrows that indicated I should go right and, lo and behold, I was free of Pontiac. Or was it free of me?

To be perfectly honest, if the weather is fine tomorrow, I might just take Interstate 55 (the express route) all the way back up to Joliet and do the road trip properly. You see, as it was raining, I didn't even have the chance to park-up anywhere, so I could take a few snaps. When I was a kid, snaps was a popular slang term for photographs, but where did it come from? You never hear people say it these days, do you?

Many sections of the old road, which still run parallel to Highway 35, have been declassified and are now overgrown with weeds. Yes. In parts, nature is reclaiming the old road. However, it is *(apparently)* legal to hike along these sections.

Shortly before I reached Pontiac, I passed two hikers, though I suspect they were far from happy. They were a young couple, from what I could see of them. Both suitably dressed for the inclement weather, and both carrying rucksacks. However, she was several yards in front of him, suggesting (to me at least) that the pair had had a falling out. Poor sods. Should I have stopped, and offered them a lift? Too late now.

Now, *that's* not a bad idea, is it? I mean. Provided the weather was good, it could be quite pleasant, hiking between the towns of the old road. But would I do it? Er, no. I like the comfort of the car too much.

Mistakes. Yep. I got lost in Wilmington, too. But that was around lunchtime, so I stopped to ask for direction, put some gas in the tank and had a couple of energy bars and a coffee. I just put $10 worth in the tank, as it was $2.75 per gallon. Man, that's expensive. And, my snack came to $5.57.

As you enter the tiny town of Odell (situated between Dwight and Pontiac), there's a sign that reads: Odell. *'A small town with a big heart, where everybody is somebody.'* Now isn't that beautiful? I think so. Sentimental old sod that I am.

Music. Unfortunately, there were very few decent tracks on the radio today. But let's face it, I spoilt you yesterday, didn't I?

Anyway. Here goes.

Roxanne: The Police.

Won't back down: Tom Petty and the Heartbreakers.

Stuck in the middle with you: Steelers Wheel.

And finally.

Sugar pie honey bunch: Unfortunately, I have no idea who sang it. Do you know? No! I did *not* say that there was a prize for getting it right. Some people. You'll be wanting jam on it next.

9:15pm. I'll see what's on the box.

FRIDAY OCTOBER 23RD

8:55am. Looking out of my second floor window (that would be the first floor back home), I see that it is gloomy, and the rain continues to fall. In this country, there's no such thing as the ground floor. It's the first floor. So. If ever you should find yourself checking into either a hotel or a motel over here, and would prefer to be installed in a ground floor room, then be sure to ask for one on the first floor.

I've just been doing a bit of editing on one of the other pages. Editing? Don't you mean, correcting all those mistakes? Yes. That's what I said. Editing. It works for me.

This motel is a little pricey for what it is, $66.36, though, in its favour, it's clean and has everything I need. It doesn't, however, have a microwave. But then, you know me and microwaves. We just don't seem to be able to get along.

As per usual, before retiring to bed, I had first to perform the task of unplugging the fridge. (Well, you know how they keep me awake otherwise.) This proved to be no easy feat, as I had first to pull forward a rather large chest of drawers, on which sat an equally large (though somewhat outdated) TV set. It was only then, that I could gain access to the damn plug. Of course, this morning, I had to put it all back again. What a performance. But it was all worth it, as I managed five hours of uninterrupted sleep.

How, on God's green earth, do people manage to get eight *solid* hours of sleep? It can't be done, I tell you. It just can't be done.

The weather (bad as it is) means (unfortunately) that I shall not be taking Interstate 55 back to Joliet, to redo yesterdays journey. No. I shall plod on, and just hope that the further south I go, the better the weather will get. Wish me luck.

Whenever I switch this contraption on (my computer) and go to Documents (which is what this is), to the right of the screen there is always a little message: Tip of the day. Today's message reads: Linked or Embedded Charts. The difference between linked and embedded charts is the location of the worksheet information. And under this, it says: Learn more......

Now, I'm no Philadelphia lawyer, or Harvard professor, though neither am I stupid, but would someone (anyone) kindly explain to me, in layman's terms, just what the fuck that means. It may as well be written in Klingon.

Unless the weather improves, the details of my road trip will be scant, to say the least. However, I'm amazed at how much I've been able to write thus far. Initially, I thought that my inadequacies (as far as computing skills were concerned) would make this attempt a complete and utter disaster. Fortunately, though my one finger stop-start-typing-technique has been the cause of much frustration, I have to say, that on the whole, the exercise has been a great success. It's almost as if someone or something were helping me. I *keep* coming up with words that ordinarily I would *never* use, though I understand (perfectly, as it happens) *exactly* what it is that I am trying to convey.

Am I boring you with this intellectual shit? Yes? .... Tough. I'm quite enjoying myself.

Breakfast was just Raisin Bran, two pieces of toast, with strawberry jam and two cups of coffee.

I thought about going back to Chenoa Family Restaurant for a big fry-up, but then thought better of it.

At some point during this trip, I'm planning on buying a pair of cowboy boots. Well, "When in Rome", as they say, though I draw the line at wearing a Stetson. Yes. I'd quite like to own a pair of cowboy boots.

9:20am. Check-out is at 11:00am. But what to do until then, that's the question.

I *could* start re-reading and editing my work thus far, but I'm in no mood to do that. I am considering keeping *that* laborious task for the final three days of my holiday, back in Dickson. Or should that be, Home?

Oh, how I could do with a secretary, a proofreader and someone skilled in the art of grammar and punctuation.

But Hey! I'm trying my best. I'm having a go. And so what, if it isn't good enough? Good enough for what? Good enough for who? I've never claimed to be a writer. All I'm doing, is putting words on a page. Nothing more.

Keith Floyd (a British chef) once said: *"Cooking, is just adding heat to food."* How the food turns out is neither here nor there. (That last sentence is mine, by the way.)

And so, my friends, my writing *'is what it is'*. Whether you love it or loath it is of no consequence.

9:50am. It's stopped raining, though the sky is as grey as….. as …..erm….*'as grey as a battleship'*? Yes. That'll do. As grey as a battleship.

Carol once told me that I could be a travel writer, though I would have to disagree with her on that point. Sorry, Carol. You see, I couldn't possibly *just* write about where I'd been and what I'd seen. No. I guess I have this *need* (as it were) to put down all the emotional shit too. Do you understand? It's all down to my internal instability, you might say.

4:50pm. Litchfield, Illinois.

In truth, I am a mere 135 miles south of Chenoa, which, as you know, was where I spent last night. Now, taking into consideration the fact that I left Chenoa before 11:00am, it's pretty pathetic for five and a half hours behind the wheel. In my defence, I did make a couple of stops, and got lost on several occasions. When I say I got lost, what I mean is, that I took *more* than one wrong turning.

But bear this in mind. Although Route 66 is *fairly* well signposted, it takes an inordinate amount of concentration to follow the route.

If one were to walk this route, why, it would be as easy as falling off a log. But, apart from having to watch the road, one's speed, the other drivers (who obviously know where they're going), and the constant bombardment of information from all the other road signs, and given that the Route 66 signs are so damn small, all one has to do is look away for a split second and one has missed one's turning. Yes. Constant vigilance is required. Basically, *'It ain't easy being a road-tripper'*. Oh, my Lord no.

Having now had my little rant, I will say this: I would much rather have problems on Route 66, than have everything go swimmingly well on the interstate. There. I've said it. Driving the old road is a very pleasurable experience.

Litchfield is far larger than any of the other towns I've stayed in over the last couple of days.

The motel, though much cheaper than I have paid of late (a mere $50), is of a far lower standard.

There is no lift in this motel, and I am on the third floor. (That's the second floor, to you.)

5:25pm. I think I'll have an early dinner, and finish this later.

To be perfectly honest, I don't think there's all that much to say.

6:50pm. In the town of Waggoner (now that's an interesting name), just 18 miles north east of here (here being Litchfield, Illinois), my road trip came to a sudden halt. There was no prior warning. The Route 66 sign, complete with pointing arrow, directed me towards a bend, no more than 200 yards ahead, and not wanting to offend the sign, I kept on driving. Unfortunately, as I rounded the bend I found myself face to face with............ with...........with............a barrier? And, across the barrier were the words, Road Closed. Well! I ask you. Is this any way to run a country? I think not.

I did an about-turn, and got onto Interstate 55. Now, I could quite easily have left the interstate several miles down the road and linked up, once again, with the old road, but I decided that I'd done enough for one day.

After studying my trusty Rand McNally road atlas (for at least thirty seconds), I concluded that it was time I left Route 66 (for now) and headed for South Dakota, and the Crazy Horse

Memorial. I calculated it to be about 900 miles, as the crow flies. But only, if like me, the crow were taking the interstate.

Even if I left at 6:00am, it would still take me until 7:00pm to get there, so, it looks like I'll be stopping somewhere along the way. Don't ask me where in the hell that's gonna be, 'cos every time I make plans to be somewhere, at some time, I always end up *at least* 200 miles from there.

Oh, yes! I stopped at the 'tiny' town of Funks Grove. And, did you know that they produce maple syrup there? No. I don't suppose you did. Well what about this one. Did you know that Al Capone (the legendary gangster) had a penchant for that Nectar of the gods and, used to travel all the way from Chicago to Funks Grove for his supply? Well, if you didn't know before, you do now. So. The next time you're down the local pub, on a quiz night and that question comes up, you'll have *me* to thank for giving you the answer.

I did take one photo while in Funks Grove, and that was of an old, run-down store.

Four miles west of Funks Grove (I *do* like that name. *'So where do you live?' 'Oh, I live in Funks Grove. Do you know it? It's quite a funky little place.'*) is the town of McLean, where I also stopped for another photo opportunity. I took a photo of a place called the Dixie Travel Plaza (Route 66 Dixie). It's a gas station-cum general store-cum diner-cum Route 66 souvenir *and* gift shop. Basically, it's all things to everyone. You know the score.

So, apart from getting lost (on several occasions), it was quite a pleasant drive, if a little intense at times. Concentrate? Concentrate? I suspect that my brain will need *at least* a month to convalesce after this trip.

Music.

Yes folks, we've got some really groovy sounds for you this evening, and we're going to kick off with:

Tears of a clown: Smokey Robinson.
Do you believe in magic?: Lovin Spoonful.
Have you seen her?: The Chi-lites.

Keep on loving you: REO Speed Wagon.
Candle in the wind: Elton John.
Can't fight this feeling anymore: Air Supply.
And finally. Two that I heard while eating dinner
Follow you, follow me: Genesis.
Who are you?: The Who. This is the theme tune to the original CSI, set in Las Vegas.

Damn! I forgot to tell you about dinner. Well listen. Just remind me in the morning. Okay? Yeah. It'll keep until the morning. I'm tired, and I really don't feel like doing any more this evening.

7:05am. Yes, folks. Today, I am early. But then, I have to be. Provided the gods are on my side (oh, please do be), I expect to be out of here and on the road by 8:00am.

Man. It's a long time since I checked out of a motel by that time. But you see, I have a deadline to keep. It is imperative that I make it to Sioux Falls, South Dakota, by nightfall. *'Imperative? Aren't we being just a tad over dramatic?'* Yeah, maybe. Okay! So it's important to me. Are you happy now? Steadily moving on. You know, some days, I *really* do worry about my mental stability. (Or should that be, lack of it?)

Sioux City is located in the south east of South Dakota (and *not* to be confused with Sioux Falls, which is where I'm heading for) and appears to be one of those areas of the country with an identity crisis.

I shall endeavour to explain.

Whilst the majority of Sioux City can be found nestling in the north west of Iowa, a small portion of it straddles the border with Nebraska. A still smaller portion (so small in fact, it's hardly worth a mention, though I doubt the inhabitants of that area would agree with me), has managed to creep across the border, and is now well ensconced in the most south easterly part of south east South Dakota. Now, that's an awful lot of souths, I think you'll agree.

I'm expecting the trip to take around nine hours, though that would be on a budget (if it's appropriate to use that term) of 60 miles per hour. Of course, if all goes well, and the interstates that I'll be using are not clogged with traffic, I *should* be able to keep up a speed of 70 miles per hour. Wish me luck.

If all goes according to plan (with my track record, it's doubtful), I can expect to be in Rapid City (which is not far from the Crazy Horse Memorial) by early Sunday afternoon. Well, I've just passed my theory test. Can I now pass the practical?

I slept pretty well last night. I went to bed around 10:15pm, and didn't wake until just after 2:00am. Fortunately, I did manage a few more hours sleep, eventually crawling out of bed just after 6:00am.

7:45am. Though I've lots more to say, I just haven't got the time right now. I'll put a few notes on the microcassette recorder while I'm in the car, and fill you in later.

8:00pm. I just got back from having dinner at Emily's Café, but I'll tell you about that later.

I haven't told you about last night's dinner, yet.

Well, just to recap (and to save you any confusion), I was in Litchfield, Illinois, if you remember.

I had dinner at another one of those all-you-can-eat places called, Mavericks Steak House, which was conveniently situated directly across from where I spent the night.

I have dined at several eateries like Mavericks, and the procedure is as follows:

You order whatever main course you desire, be it steak, chicken, or fish. This then comes with a choice of potato, or rice and a bread roll, or Texas toast. I plumped for the *extra* thick steak (rare) with rice and Texas toast. After that, it's simply a case of all-you-can-eat, from the extensive variety of both hot and cold foods, from the buffet. After that, there's a large selection of desserts to help yourself to.

With my steak, rice and toast, I had a *very* large plate of salad. And, after polishing all that off, I had some apple and cinnamon sponge, banana custard (now when did I last eat anything like that?) and a biscuit. Wash all that lot down with a glass of Pepsi, and what do you find? That the world isn't such a bad place after all. And all for the princely sum of $13.60, plus a $4 tip. Well. I was feeling generous.

For marks out of ten. It has to be an 8.

So. Am I in Sioux Falls? No. But, I am only 30 miles away. '*So, what was wrong with driving another 30 miles?*' you ask. Well, let's just say, that it was all down to my miscalculation.

A word of advice. *Never,* use your finger as a guide when calculating distance in miles.

I seem to recall saying (though as it's late, I can't be bothered to scroll back and confirm it) that it was approximately 600 miles from Litchfield, Illinois, to Sioux Falls, South Dakota. However, my calculations were out by 70 miles. (1) That's at least an hour extra driving, and (2) I couldn't possibly have known that I would be slowed up (several times) by roadworks. What I thought would be, at best, an eight hour drive and, at worst, a nine hour drive, did in fact, turn out to be closer to ten and a half hours, and I didn't even reach my original destination.

So here I am, spending the night 30 miles south of Sioux Falls, in a little town called Beresford. And do you want to know something? I'm bloody glad I did stop here. Wait'll you hear this.

I walked into this motel (a Super 8) and asked for a room for one night. The owner, an Indian (not the native American kind) called Yogesh Amin (though better known as Yogi) asked if I had a reservation (but you know me, I never make a reservation, I just show up), and I said *'No'*. After asking whether I required smoking, or non smoking, he informed me that he only had one room left, and it was a smoking room. Initially, I said *'No thanks'* and was about to turn around and walk out, but it was already getting dark (which was why I stopped driving when I did), so I asked if I could just walk into the room and find out whether it was particularly smokey, or not. Yogi agreed. And, although there was that distinct smell of cigarette smoke, I thought to myself, *'It's only one night'*. Yogi told me that it would normally cost $65, plus tax, but as it was the last room, and as I was a non-smoker putting up with a smokey room, he would only charge me $55, plus tax, and the total would be $59-68. Bargain.

So now it's time to pay. First, I place my American express traveller's cheque on the counter, and then I offer him my British Passport. At this, his eyes lit up. *"You're British!",* he says. (God only knows what he thought I was before that.) *"Yes."* I replied.

Then, he tells me that he had lived in Brixton for 27 years. We chat about England for a while, and he decides to upgrade me to a suite. But how can he do this, if he is already giving me the last room? Simple. The hot tub (Jacuzzi) in one of the suites is broken, consequently, he is not letting that particular room out. But, provided I don't use the hot tub, I'm welcome to have the room.

I enter my suite. To the right there is a small closet, with a sink. Past that, there is a bathroom with a sink, a toilet and a bath with shower attachment. I retrace my steps, and I'm back at the door. Now, I walk towards my living room, but before I reach it, to my right I find a small kitchen area, with sink, fridge, microwave and storage cupboards, on top of which I find a coffee maker and a selection of teas and coffees. Moving on, I enter my living room, where I find a large sofa, a chest of drawers (on which, sits a plasma screen TV), a coffee table and a writing table, with two chairs. The double doors, which lead to my *large* bedroom are already open and, apart from a double bed, there is another chest of drawers on which sits another TV set. Yes. I've got two TV's. And, in my *very large* bedroom there is a humongous hot tub (shame it's not working), with a shower next to it. And what am I paying for all this luxury? Oh! That's right. I've already told you. It's an upgrade. It's a mere $59.68. Doesn't it just restore your faith in human nature?

Yogi told me that, if ever I'm around this way again, I can have another discount.

Now, apart from my miscalculations (and the roadworks), I only took one wrong turn, and I soon corrected my mistake.

On Leaving Litchfield, I headed south on Interstate 55, until I reached St Louis. There, I joined Interstate 70 for a short while, before transferring to Interstate 270. Interstate 270 took me from east to west across the northern part of St Louis, where it again linked up with Interstate 70. Once back on Interstate 70, it was a straight run across Missouri, all the way to Kansas City, which straddles Kansas and Missouri. After travelling a short distance along Highway 71 (in Kansas City) I then joined Interstate 29, which brought me straight up to where I am now.

Now. If my calculations are right, and if the town of Sioux Falls is indeed a mere 300 miles from Rapid City, then it should be no more than a six hour trip. Which means, that for me to be there by 3:00pm, I shouldn't have to leave here until 9:00am.

10:30pm. I'm tired. But, I guess I can have a lie-in tomorrow.

Somewhere along Interstate 70 (in Missouri, I think), I saw a sign that read:

YOU DRINK.
YOU DRIVE.
YOU DIE.

Short and sweet, but straight to the point. No? Why do we sometimes write No with a question mark, when what we really mean is yes? I guess I could change it, but it amuses me.

Autobahns. Now I can't remember the name of the American president during world war two, but I do know that he was so impressed with Hitler's network of autobahns, that it prompted him to introduce a massive road-building programme, culminating in the introduction of what we now know as Interstates. Which begs the question: Had it not been for Hitler's autobahns, would Route 66 (and many other roads like it) still be a main highway?

Ironic, really. For, were it not for the introduction of the interstate (or "super slab" as Jerry McClanahan describes it), Route 66 would not be as famous as it is. (Jerry McClanahan is the author of the EZ66 guide for travellers and an authority on the history of Route 66) No. It would be just another road. As the saying goes: *'You never know what you've got 'til it's gone'*. Yep. In the case of Route 66, it had to be lost before it could be found. And now that it is found, long may it be cherished, never to be lost again. Amen.

When I was still on Interstate 270, I saw a sign for Interstate 55, with Memphis on it. And, I have to admit, I was sorely tempted to jump on it (figuratively speaking) and head south for some sun. But.........Oh, I don't know.

11:10pm. It's no good. I'm just too darn tired. I'll give you the music info in the morning. So. It's good night, and don't wake me up.

7:50am. Well, although (as per usual) I woke up several times during the night, I had no trouble in getting back to sleep and, I'm pleased to inform you that that was the best night's sleep I've had since I arrived.

Of course, tiredness could have played a large part in my sudden need for more sleep. Having said that, over ten hours behind the wheel, with just three stops (two to refuel and one to eat a bag of pretzels and study the map) and a distance of 640 miles covered, *could* have played a big part in it. Could it not?

However, there's no substitute for quality. Even the towels in this room are whiter than the ones in my last motel.

In Litchfield, I observed the towels to be somewhere between, off-white and grey. The sink had obviously been leant on at some point, consequently, there was a crack between it and the wall. No matter how hard I tried, I couldn't get the bath tap to stop dripping.

The room had neither fridge nor microwave (not that that bothered me). What *did*, however, cause me some concern, was the safe in the corner. As you know, I have already stayed in motels that provide safes in their rooms. However, this particular safe was of the key operated variety, as opposed to the digital variety. So, I headed down to reception and enquired about a key. *"No key"*, was the reply. *"But there is a safe in the corner of my room, and I wish to deposit my travellers' cheques and passport into it for safe keeping."* (no pun intended) *"It's okay. Nobody goes in the rooms"*, he replied. I gave him my best baffled look, and walked away, shaking my head. What kind of a place was this, that they could provide a safe, that in reality, was nothing more than a redundant piece of furniture. Maybe they could put a cloth over it and put a vase of flowers on top. Or, maybe I should drag a chair over to the window, rest my coffee cup on the safe and just watch the world go by. Yeah. Right. The day one of these rooms gets broken into, the occupant will sue the arse off this company. Well, you know how much they love a good lawsuit in this country.

Before checking out of the Litchfield motel, I had breakfast. No Raisin Bran, unfortunately. I had to settle for a bowl of Rice Krispies. Now *there's* a blast from the past.

The Rice Krispies were followed by a toasted muffin, that, although toasted *three times,* no less, and though it was both hot and of a toast like consistency, refused to go brown. This I had with butter and jam. Oh! And I mustn't forget the icing-sugar-coated doughnut. The coffee was weak and not dissimilar to hot water.

Between the fridge and one of the cupboards was some kind of a trap, though I did not get close enough to ascertain whether it was for small rodents, or cockroaches.

All in all, the motel, like so many others I've had the misfortune to stay at, wasn't well maintained. Pity.

Dinner (last night) was later than usual, for reasons I have already explained, and was taken at Emily's Café.

Now *that's* something that just blows my mind. How does the computer know to put an accent over the "e", in Café? It'll probably tell me in a minute. You just wait and see.

Emily's. A nice enough place to eat, though the food wasn't as hot as it should have been. (By, not hot enough, I don't mean chilli heat hot. No. The food was only warm. No. It's no good arguing. You'll have to be marked down for that, I'm afraid). I opted for the chilli, which came with crackers and a small container of sour cream. Now, although I've never tried sour cream, and wasn't too sure what I should do with it, I simply mixed it in with my chilli, which, I have to admit, was a perfect accompaniment to the dish, even at the cost of cooling down my food even more.

The chilli was followed by the Deluxe Chicken Sandwich, though I failed to see what was so deluxe about it. It was a large bread roll, containing chargrilled chicken, bacon, salad and, I suspect, mayonnaise. Again. What made it deluxe? Perhaps it was those three small pieces of pickled gherkin that were strategically positioned on the plate, just to the side of my sandwich. Who knows?

I had a glass of Pepsi, and the bill came to $10.06. So so. The waitress was pleasant enough, so I left her $3.

Out of ten? Just a 6………sadly.

Oddly enough, on this road trip, I haven't had the misfortune of getting stressed over whether or how many postcards to send. However I have decided that I will *probably* send a few when I reach Rapid City. No. Scratch that. Better make that, *If* I reach Rapid City.

It's 9:15am, and I was supposed to be out of here by 9:00am. Oh. *'The best laid plans of mice and men'*, as they say.

Oh, what the fuck. I'll get there when I get there.

If I have to leave the laundry until tomorrow morning, so what? I won't be checking out until Tuesday morning, so it'll have all day Monday to air.

Music from Saturday:

Go back Jack: Steely Dan (I think).

One of these nights: The Eagles.

Crocodile Rock: Elton John.

Love Shack: The B52s.

Only the good die young: (well that's just depressed me) Billy Joel.

Best day of my life: Dido.

I'm going through changes: Ozzy Osbourne.

In the air tonight: Phil Collins.

Maggie May: Rod Stewart.

Born to be wild: (great song) Steppenwolf.

In the city: (theme tune to a movie called, The Warriors) The Eagles.

Under my thumb: The Rolling Stones.

Life in the fast lane: The Eagles.

Revolution: (excellent) The Beatles.

The logical song: Supertramp.

Young Americans: David Bowie.

All along the watch tower: The inimitable, Jimmy Hendrix.

Time after time: (beautiful song) Cindy Lauper.

Wonderful tonight: Eric Clapton.

Man eater: Hall and Oates.

And finally. One of the greatest song ever written. And, I might add, my second favourite song. Yes. It's............

Two out of three ain't bad: Meatloaf. Need I say more? If you've never heard it, then why not listen to it on YouTube? I always start filling up when I hear that song. But, enough of that.

Before I go, I've just got time to tell you about breakfast.

No. I won't bore you with those details. After all, it was nothing to write home about.

9:35am. Time to get packed up.

I'll race you to Rapid City. The last one there pays for the room, okay?

4:15pm. I made it! I'm in Rapid City. The motel is absolutely amazing, if that isn't overstating it just a little. No. Of course it isn't. I wouldn't say it if I didn't mean it.

I've gained an hour, as I have just crossed another one of those time zones, my laundry is happily swimming around in the warm water of the washing machine, this wonderful room in this equally wonderful motel is costing me a mere $49.74 per night and, although my car is playing up (more on that later), I have already been in touch with Avis in Nashville, who suggested I take my vehicle to Rapid City Airport, where they will either service it or replace it. Now that's got to be one of the longest sentences in the history of the written word, wouldn't you agree? Oh, just nod your head, and let me do the talking.

Just out of curiosity I decided to do a bit of digging, and see if I could find out what was actually the longest sentence in the world. Sadly, mine isn't even close. Are you ready for this? I think you'd better sit down, this is going to come as a bit of a shock. The longest sentence in the world can be found in a book called *The Rotters Club*, by Jonathan Coe, and contains 13955 words. Doesn't it just make you sick? Never mind. I'll just stick to what

I'm good at……when I eventually find out what that is……if I find out what that is.

If I were to make one criticism of this motel, it would be the $1.12 per day for the use of the safe in my room. Of course, the charge *is* optional. However, should you choose not to pay and the safe be broken into (and all your valuables stolen) then the motel would not be liable. So. On reflection. I don't *really* mind.

Ah! 4:35pm. My laundry should be just about cooked by now. Better go and put it in the dryer.

Right! That's all sorted. I'll go back in about 20 minutes time.

After saying farewell to Yogi, I checked out of the motel in Beresford, South Dakota and headed north on Interstate 29, in the direction of Sioux Falls. It being Sunday, the road was quiet, so I accelerated up to 75 miles per hour (and yes, that is the speed limit in that particular state), switched to cruise control and just sat back and enjoyed the scenery.

Sorry. Nearly forgot. (what do you mean, *nearly*?) After checking out (but before leaving town) I went across the street to gas up. And I'm glad I did. You see, I discovered that there is a cheaper fuel that can be used in my car. A whole ten cents a gallon cheaper, in fact. The fuel is simply called Super Unleaded, as opposed to the regular unleaded *and*, here's the good thing about it (could there be anything better than it being ten cents cheaper?), it's better for the environment. Now isn't that good?

Okay. Laundry is washed, dried and is now neatly laid out on the bed, airing.

I've just had a word with the lady at reception, and enquired about the price, should I decide to stay for an extra night. Right now, it's Sunday and I'm booked in until Tuesday morning, however, I think I might need an extra night here. She informed me that it would *probably* be the same, but it would be best if I checked in the morning. That's the only problem with motels. The prices can vary from day to day.

5:45pm. Dinner.

7:15pm. About 90 miles east of Rapid City I was overtaken by an SUV (Sports Utility Vehicle), on top of which (firmly strapped down, I hoped), was a dead deer. Of course, out here it's quite a common sight, I would imagine.

8:25pm. Well that was a stroke of luck. Whilst sitting here, trying to think of something to say, and then actually put the words in the correct order, I glanced over to my left, where all the guest information sits neatly in a plastic desktop stand and I spotted a leaflet about High Speed Wireless Internet, 'A User's Guide'. Well, I won't bore you with all the details, save-to-say, I decided to go down to reception and have a chat with the young lady about it. Unfortunately, like me, she knew little about the wonders of wireless Internet. However, a guy she was talking to (her boyfriend, I think) knew just about all there was to know, and within minutes of pressing a few buttons on my computer, lo and behold, not only was I able to access the Internet, I was also able to send emails. Of course, if and when I switch my beloved computer off, and then turn it on again, I may just have a spot of bother when it comes to pressing the right buttons. I did, however, manage to write down *some* of the information he gave me, so maybe I'll be able to figure the rest out for myself. Well, here's hoping.

Back to Interstate 90. Five miles further down the road (85 miles east of Rapid City) I saw a sign that read: Bear Country. U S A. And what picture do you suppose they put on this sign? A bear? No. A Mountain Lion. Hey! Maybe they couldn't find a picture of a bear.

Some days, I'm convinced that this is *all* just a bad dream. Or should that be. Nightmare?

I dined at Outback Steakhouse, a restaurant I could *see* on my last visit to Rapid City, but could not find my way to. *'Explain!'* I hear you cry.

It was Sunday, October 15th, 2006 and I was staying at Motel 6, which is just across the interstate from where I am now. I remembered having a really good meal at an Outback Steakhouse

75

in Secaucus, New Jersey, back in 2004, so I thinks to myself *'yeah, that'll do for me'*. However, after crossing the interstate and trying in vain to find the damn place (which, incidentally, is closeted behind Econo Lodge), I had to settle for a meal in Bostons Sports Bar, where, I might add, I encountered yet another waitress who tried to use psychology on me to get a larger tip. But, you know what they say: *'Once bitten, twice shy'*. Or, there's the saying that George W Bush managed to fuck up: *'Fool me once, shame on you. Fool me twice, shame on me'*. Poor old George. He only managed to get the *'Fool me once'*, out. The rest was just gobbledygook. And before you ask. Yes. That word *is* in the dictionary.

Well, you'll be pleased to know that, after switching my computer off then switching it back on again, I successfully managed to get back onto the Internet. *Yes!* There's just no stopping this boy.

Hey! Sorry about that. I got sidetracked.

I was telling you about Outback, wasn't I?

Although, on this occasion, I did actually find the place, I drove past the entrance twice before realizing my mistake.

The restaurant, though dimly lit, was nevertheless extremely well patronized. I started with the 'blooming onion'. This (obviously) is an onion, which has been hand carved (so it says on the menu) and splayed (so it resembles a hedgehog) and then, somehow, is lightly battered and deep fried. This is then served with a (what I would describe as) tangy Marie Rose sauce. (That would be prawn cocktail sauce to you.) Did I tell you that I used to be in catering? Well I was. So there!

It was a really tasty starter, though too large for one. By that, I mean that I had trouble finishing my main course.

Yes. The main course. This was chargrilled chicken, topped with mushrooms, bacon, honey mustard sauce and melted cheese. Not bad, but a little heavy on the seasoning (too salty). The chicken came with fries and a selection of vegetables, which included, courgette, carrot, broccoli and mangetout. And, with two glasses of coke, the whole meal came to $24.97. Pricey. Somehow, I don't think I'll be going back. I left $30, which does make it rather a large tip. (About 20%, by my calculations) And my score for the evening? Well, that would have to be 6/10.

10:10pm. I'm tired now, and I want to watch some telly. Goodnight.

The Crazy Horse Memorial, South Dakota.

What the Crazy Horse Memorial will look like on completion.

5:50am. I've been up since 4:30am, *trying* (without much success) to gain access to my Wyndham Rewards account. I *did* (as I always do) key in the correct password, as I know the damn thing by heart. However, Wyndhams, in their infinite wisdom (he said sarcastically), kept telling me that I had made an error, and that I should try again. Well, after much cursing and swearing I conceded defeat, pressed the button for Forgotten Your Password?, making me look like an idiot, when all the time it was *their* mistake, not mine. Anyway. The upshot is, that I am missing reward points from no less than *five* motels out of the *ten* I have stayed at thus far. Did I tell you that *'It's no easy life being a road tripper'?* Oh, crikes no.

8:05am. As last night's dinner was still laying heavy on my stomach, I decided on a light breakfast of cereal (don't ask me what kind it was, as I'd never seen the likes before in my life. They were just little, golden, square, crunchy things) and two cups of coffee.

I've checked in for another night. (That's an extra night, not tonight) Yes. I shall be here until Wednesday.

I'd better think about getting off to the airport, to sort this car out. Oh, how I hope they swap it for one with less miles on the clock. When I took delivery of this vehicle, it had already been driven over 20,000 miles. I myself have increased that by a further 3,500 miles, so you could say that it has taken a bit of a hammering.

Rapid City Airport is no more than 12 miles away, so *providing* I don't get lost, I should be there and back in no time. Wish me luck.

10:30am. *'The job's a good-un'.*

Though (not surprisingly) I missed the turning for the airport, I only drove approximately half a mile down the road before realizing my mistake, which was soon corrected with a three (make that five) point turn.

Unfortunately, Avis had no cars that gave the same kind of mileage as my Chevy Cobalt. So, the guy directed me to the garage where they have their vehicles serviced. Rapid Lube, on East Omaha Street, which, by the way, is nothing more than a hop, skip and a jump away from my motel.

The service itself was a mere $34.93, which, although I had to pay, I will be reimbursed for when I return the car to Nashville.

I've just been checking my records and, the same thing happened to me on November 3rd, 2006. Back then, I was in Stockbridge, Georgia and the service cost me $23.84. Now, if I didn't keep records, you wouldn't have known that, would you? Yeah. Like you really care.

Whilst waiting for the car to be serviced, or whatever it is they do, I helped myself to a coffee. Hey! The service only took those guys about ten minutes. It's amazing. Makes me wish I knew more about cars.

Now that puts me in mind of Donald Sutherland (father of Keifer Sutherland), who played *Oddball*, a tank commander in the brilliant (and I have to say, one of my favourite movies) Kelly's Heroes, which also starred Clint Eastwood and Telly Savalas. Savalas? Not too sure if I've spelt that correctly, but I'm sure he'll forgive me.

Anyway. When one of the tanks broke down, and it was *'all hands to the pumps'*, as it were, *Oddball* was just sat there, *'drinking wine, eating cheese and getting some rays'*, as he put it. And, when asked why he wasn't helping out, he simply replied: *"Oh, I don't know anything about tanks, man. I just ride 'em."* Genius. Pure genius. I'm laughing to myself just thinking about it. If you've never seen the movie, then I would strongly recommend it. Did it come out in 1970, or was it 1971? It's immaterial. All you need to know is that it's a bloody good movie.

But what's all this got to do with me? Well. *"I don't know anything about cars, man. I just drive 'em."*

On the way back to the motel, I spotted a Walgreens. They sell all kinds of good stuff in Walgreens, and you'll find them all over America. I guess the equivalent back home would be Boots. Until I got this new digital camera, I would often get my films processed at Walgreens. Of course, I may still need to get the odd 'four by six', for Stella and Orville, back in Dickson. Stella usually asks for a copy of either this one or that one. You know.

The reason I stopped in at Walgreens, was to buy some antiseptic cream for my toe. Several days ago (somehow or other) I sustained a small cut on one of my toes, but thought nothing of it. Now, however, it has become inflamed and is causing me some discomfort. Hence the antiseptic cream.

It was as I was walking into Walgreens, that I realized something was missing. Back at the service centre, I'd left the bag containing my road atlas, glasses, motel books and my umbrella. Can you imagine anything worse than that? An Englishman without his umbrella. Had I not recovered my umbrella, why, I would surely have needed counselling for months, if not years.

As I walked into the service centre, one of the mechanics was just about to put the bag in the office. And so, the fragile balance of life was once again restored.

11:45am. Though the sun is shining, it's still chilly out there. Should I go to the Crazy Horse Memorial today? Maybe I'll leave it until tomorrow.

Hey! That's what I was going to do. Postcards! Dreaded postcards. Fortunately, they just happen to have a rack full of them in the lobby. I already have plenty of stamps. I bought twenty of them, while still in Dickson. But. Before that. *'What happened to yesterday's music?'* I hear you cry. Oh, well. If you insist.

Yellow Brick Road: Elton John.

You're Beautiful: (and a beautiful song it is too) James Blunt.

Come together: The Beatles.

Blinded by the light: Manfred Mann. (Did you know that that song was written by Bruce Springsteen? You do now.)

Sugar Sugar: The Archies (or is it Archy's?)

Honky tonk woman: The Rolling Stones.

We gotta get out of this place: The Animals.

What would you say?: Hurricane Smith. (Now, when was the last time you heard that song? Come on. I'm waiting.)

Working my way back to you: Frankie Valli and the Four Seasons.

Imagine: John Lennon.
Daydream Believer: The Monkees.
You've lost that lovin' feeling: The Righteous Brothers.
And last, but not least, it's:
Who's gonna drive you home?: The Cars.

Well, that completes yesterday's line-up, and I hope you've learnt something from it. And, if you haven't, well, I'm no teacher, so you can hardly blame *me*.

7:40pm. Now, what's that saying? *'See Venice and Die'?* Or is it, *'See Florence and die'?* Damned if I know. It's no good asking me, I'm only here to make up the numbers 'cos they were one short. Well, I don't care what the saying is. Listen, while I tell you this. Sorry for the break in transmission but, in the last five minutes, I've just composed a little Ditty. I shall not call it a poem at this stage, as it requires much more work than I have time to put into it at this juncture.

The Crazy Horse Memorial
Forget the Eiffel Tower
With its spikey pointy bit,
The Taj Mahal so shiney white
We've seen enough of it.

The Pyramids are old hat now
They really are a bore,
Miss Liberty the statue?
I've seen it all before.

But there's one sight you must all see
On me you can depend,
The Crazy Horse Memorial
Is where *my* time will end.

October 26th 2009
Brendan J. A. O'Leary

Now, be honest. You've read worse. No! I'm not asking you. I'm *telling* you. You've read worse. Okay. Fair enough. *I've* read worse.

Yes. You guessed it. I went to the Crazy Horse Memorial. Unfortunately, I went a little late, so I didn't spend as much time there as I would have liked. No matter! I'm going again in the morning. You can come too, if you like. Oh, no. Wait a minute. You can't. Can you? 'Cos you're not here.

But seriously. If you only take one more trip abroad in your life, I urge you to visit South Dakota and the Crazy Horse Memorial. I'll say no more on the subject. Well. Probably not.

Damn. I've just had a thought. I'll have to talk about it again, as I'm going back there in the morning.

Three years ago, I had dinner at the Millstone Restaurant. And, although I can't remember what I had for main, I *do* recall having the chocolate brownie, with cream and ice cream.

This evening, I dined there again. I started with the ham and bean soup, and a plate of lettuce, sweetcorn salad, bean salad, potato salad, pasta salad and grated cheese. Then came the main. I had the 10 ounce sirloin, with baked potato and garlic bread. This came with a small container of butter and a sachet of sour cream. I've been eating far too much just lately, so I passed on the salad dressing. Well, even *I* make sacrifices, from time to time.

TUESDAY OCTOBER 27ᵀᴴ

7:30am. Though I would dearly love to go back to the Crazy Horse Memorial today, looking at the weather forecast earlier, it said that it would be windy and the temperature may be as low as 60 degrees. No. Not really a day for wandering around outside. But, it's still early and not quite light out yet.

The Millstone. Though the food was good, it wasn't hot enough. What's the point of serving a baked jacket potato, if it's only warm? The butter simply will not melt when spread onto the potato's interior.

My steak, though well cooked (rare), lacked seasoning. My God! I'm starting to talk like one of the judges from Master Chef. Somebody! Please! Save me from myself!

It's a shame, but I'm afraid the Millstone only gets 6/10. Had the food been hotter, it would most certainly have received an 8.

Obviously, I didn't do much driving yesterday, just the 75 mile round trip to see Crazy Horse. Oh! There was the 30 mile round trip to the airport, but, at the end of the day, and when all's said and done………I've lost my train of thought now. Oh, yes! I'm afraid there was nothing of any interest to report on the music front. Until, that is, I was eating dinner. Oh, yes. *Then,* I was fortunate enough to hear three really *great* songs.

Homeward Bound: Simon and Garfunkel. (Sorry. Not too sure about the spelling of that last name.)

Happy just to dance with you: The Beatles. The lead vocalist on this track (as any Beatles fan worth his salt will know) was George Harrison. And those of you who didn't, well shame on you.

And finally. I haven't a clue who sang this song (shame on me?), but it is:

Born too late: I'm only guessing, but I'd say that the song came out in either the late fifties, or early sixties.

A Rant and a Road Trip

Perhaps one of the more mature people reading this rubbish, might just be able to help me out with this song. Do you think? You know the routine by now. *'Answers on a postcard. Please!'*

6:45pm. I've just arrived back, after dining at Red Lobster. But more of that later.

Yes. I went back to the Crazy Horse Memorial. Far more than just a place from which to view the mountain (that in as little as thirty years, could well be the finished article), The Crazy Horse Memorial is a massive complex, with buildings displaying artefacts of Native American culture, a small theatre that shows a documentary about the conception and then realization of the whole project, the artist's studio (with much of his work still in it) and a large restaurant.

When completed, the sculpture of the mighty Crazy Horse will look down not only on the existing buildings, but also, on a university, and medical centre, which I believe will be for the benefit of the local Native Americans. It should be an amazing spectacle.

So who was this sculptor, commissioned to create the largest sculpture in the world? His name was Korczak Ziolkowski. A self-taught artist and sculptor, born in Boston, on September 6th, 1908 and died on October 20th, 1982. And his name? Well. He was of Polish descent.

It was in 1939, after winning first prize for his sculpture, PADEREWSKI: 'Study of an Immortal', at the New York World Fair, that Korczak Ziolkowski first came to the attention of Lakota Chief, Henry Standing Bear.

It wasn't until 1947 that Korczak arrived in the Black Hills. May 3rd, to be precise. He then started work on what many believe will not only be the largest sculpture in the world, but the greatest man-made structure of all time. And yes. That includes me.

Now, before we go any further, it has recently come to my attention, that it is neither Florence, nor Venice. No. The actual saying is: *'See Naples and die'*. I'm so glad we got that cleared up.

85

Korczak was nearly 40 years old when he started this mammoth project, and knew that he would never live to see its completion. However, his wife (Ruth) and seven of their ten children, are devoted to seeing it through to the end.

It was in 1948 that Korczak started work on the mountain. After seeing pictures of what has been achieved thus far, I (in my ignorance) calculated that it would *probably* take at least another 100 years to complete the project. But, as a bus driver at the centre informed me, advances in technology mean that it could well be finished in as little as 30 year's time.

Now, those of you who know me well, know that I am no great lover of this planet, or the majority of the people who inhabit it. So, when my time has come, my number is up and it is time to shuffle off this mortal coil, I shall not be wishing that I could stay just a *little* longer. However, after being privileged enough to gaze upon such a wonder as this, I should dearly love to see its completion.

So. Forget Naples, or Florence, or whatever it is, and get your arse over here and see what I would class as number one, in the eight wonders of the world.

Am I having a rant? When am I not having one?

So. Dinner at Red Lobster.

As the name suggests, they specialize in seafood.

Odd, really. I mean, in all the years I've been coming to this country, and all the Red Lobsters I've seen, this is the first one I've dined at. I very nearly ate at one in Anderson, Indiana, several years ago, but on seeing how busy the place was, I decided to give it a miss.

My heart sang when I saw that they had Gumbo on the menu. Now, for those of you who do not know what gumbo is, I shall give you a brief description. It's prawns, chicken and vegetables in (what I would describe as) a mild, creamy, curry sauce. I've only ever had it once before, which was several years ago, in Milford, Pennsylvania. The memory of that delectable bowl of food will stay with me forever. 10/10.

Red Lobster's gumbo? I'll be generous and let them have 7/10. To be perfectly honest, it was only between a 6 and a 7.

My main course was the baked Tilapia, topped with garlic shrimp (for shrimp, read prawn) and salsa, accompanied by broccoli and a savoury rice.

The fish was over-seasoned, though succulent and tasty. Oh! There's Master Chef again.

I had two glasses of coke, and the bill (they say check, over here) came to $25.15. No. Far too much for what it was. Still. I felt obliged to leave $30.

As for the décor. Well, the interior was mainly wood and, while the dark, varnished parts gave one the impression of being inside a beautiful, old sailing ship, the unvarnished timber gave one the impression of being inside an old, wooden hut on a quayside. Sad. But true.

Red Lobster. Not an experience I shall be repeating. Well. Not in Rapid City.

After arriving back at the motel, I nipped to the gas station next door, for a paper and an FVC. Ah! Luxury.

Hey! A picture of me just appeared on the right hand side of the screen. It was the one where I'm holding an M16 assault rifle, and doing my damnedest to look mean. Now then. Was that 2001? No. No it wasn't. It's coming back to me now. That picture was taken at the Gun Store, on Tropicana Avenue, Las Vegas, in 2002. Now what was that song Lennon once sang, *'Happiness is a warm gun'*? Hm. Yes. I believe it was. Now then, if you are a pacifist, I hope you can forgive me for saying this, but firing that powerful weapon gave me one hell of a buzz. Wow. Must do it again, sometime.

Me, at the Crazy Horse Memorial.

7:45am. Well. I've showered, brushed my teeth, had breakfast (same as yesterday: cornflakes, a toasted muffin with butter and two cups of coffee. Ah! Yesterday, I also had an apple.), just about finished packing and I'm ready for the off. I'll shave this evening, when I reach my destination (wherever that's going to be). Yep. Your guess is as good as mine on that one.

The poem I wrote a couple of days ago has been expanded by one verse. However, I *am* in the process of creating another along the same lines, though far more serious.

I might as well give you the updated version:

<u>The Crazy Horse Memorial</u>
They say you should see Naples,
And then turn up your toes.
The Leaning Tower of Pisa,
Though why, God only knows.

Forget the Eiffel Tower,
With its pointy, spiky bit.
The Taj Mahal all gleaming white,
I've seen enough of it.

The Pyramids are old hat now,
And really quite a bore.
Miss Liberty the statue?
I've seen it all before.

But there's one place that you *must* see.
On me you can depend.
The Crazy Horse Memorial,
Is where *my* time will end.

Hey! That's spooky. Just as I finished the last line of that poem, the picture on the right hand side of my screen was of the Sphinx in front of the Luxor Hotel, in Las Vegas. For those of you who don't know, The Luxor Hotel is in the shape of a pyramid. You don't suppose that my reference to the pyramids being a bit old hat has upset anyone, do you? No. Surely not. Hey! Come on. I mean, it's not like I broke into a tomb, or anything like that.

IF! And I mean *IF.* If I can complete the more serious poem (which is well under way and obviously has references to both Korczak and Crazy Horse), I shall send copies of them to Ruth. That's Korczak's wife, who, incidentally, I just happened to catch a glimpse of only yesterday, before she slipped through one of the doors into a private section of the complex. I was just taking a picture of the scaled-down model of the Crazy Horse Memorial, when I saw her out of the corner of my eye. Unfortunately, by the time I turned to my right, she was just disappearing through the open door. Never mind.

Souvenirs. APU (as per usual), I bought some fridge magnets for myself and for my sister, Anne. Oh, how we love our fridge magnets. So. The next time you're on holiday, and you feel that you just *have* to buy a present for a friend, or family member, then just remember this, you can't go far wrong with a fridge magnet. Oh, crumbs no. After all. Everyone has a fridge, don't they?

Oh, you're not going to believe this, but it's snowing. Yes. I've just glanced out the window, in the vain hope of seeing the sun, and what pitiful sight should greet me? Now, just you hold your horses there, I haven't finished yet. Although, at present, it's only light and has not yet stuck to the ground, it is, unfortunately, coming down horizontally. Which means, that it's bloody cold and very windy out there. Question: Should I stay another night in Rapid City? What if the snow sticks, making it more difficult to leave town in the morning? What then? Stay yet another night? Oh! You know how I hate making decisions. Could one of you people at least *try* to help me out here? Is that *too* much to ask? Well, if that's your attitude, then I'm not going to let you read my book. Yes! I said book. Because? Because I've decided that that's what it is. Okay?

Steadily moving on. It's still snowing. Oh, bollocks.

I also purchased some more postcards, though these were mainly for my own personal collection. One day, I may just cover a complete wall with my collection. What was that? How many have I got? Oh, I would say, about 250 (and rising).

I usually buy a little something for my friend Trudy. And this year was no exception. I bought her *another* Thunderbird necklace. Yes. I bought her two Thunderbird necklaces last year. Well! She likes Thunderbird. What more can I say.

Thunderbird. One of many native American symbols. It is (obviously) the shape of a bird and is the *'Sacred Bearer of Happiness'*. Hey! I didn't come up the river on a bicycle, you know. I *do* know a bit.

Should I go down to Lubbock, Texas and call in on Trish (Mrs Angry Head) at the Buddy Holly Centre? I wonder if she's still mad at me. Don't ask. It's a long story, involving a goldfish, a vacuum cleaner and a packet of digestive biscuits. Still. Could be worse. Could be snowing. *DOH!*

9:10am. Sod it. I'll hit the road.

8:25pm. I don't feel much like writing at the moment, but I must persevere.

Well. Am I happy? I guess I am (in a way).

I just finished an email to Hannah. Yes! You heard me. I emailed her a photo of me at the Crazy Horse Memorial, not expecting her to reply. However, when I arrived back, after dining at the truck stop across the road, I switched on my computer, went straight to my messages (as I always do) and lo and behold, there *was* a message from Hannah. Yes. I have to say, it made my day.

The only fly in the ointment (as it were), is that there is a problem with the out-going server, consequently, although I've written her another email and pushed the send button, it hasn't gone. But, she's okay, and that's all that matters.

Originally, I *had* planned to stay at the Super 8 motel, about four miles north of where I am right now. Unfortunately, as that particular motel was more than three miles from the interstate and I got lost, I was forced to abandon my search and request directions (from two charming souls) *back* to the interstate, where I simply headed further south and checked into this establishment, just spitting distance from the interstate. Oh, I do like to be able to see a highway, or the interstate. Don't you?

No. I'm sorry. I just can't do this tonight. I'm dog tired and I want to watch the box for a change. *Stop moaning!* I'll see you in the morning. People, eh?

8:35am. I'm having a few problems with the computer at the moment. No. Not the computer exactly, more the server. (Yeah! Like I understand what I'm talking about.) Apparently, although I'm actually on the Internet, I can't send emails. Let's just hope that things are different in Joplin, Missouri, this evening.

When I received a reply to the email I had sent to Hannah, the computer requested I confirm receipt of her email, so she would know that it had indeed arrived. Unfortunately, every time I checked to see if the problem had been fixed, my machine informed me that it had not.

After confirming receipt of her email, I sent Hannah another, much longer email. However, that too is still in the system, waiting like a delayed passenger at the airport for someone to tell him when, if ever, the damn plane is going to take off.

I'm thousands of miles away from the postal strike back home, yet I understand fully the frustrations of those awaiting mail.

Still. Must be positive. Things *will* be different, once I reach Joplin.

Motels. I could live in a motel.

My room (simply furnished though it may be) has everything I need. It is my bedroom-cum-living room-cum kitchen-cum-office, complete with en suite facilities. What more could I want?

It's so uncomplicated to be able to crawl out of bed, step into the shower and wash away the night's sleep.

A shower is not merely a means by which one cleanses oneself. No. It also has therapeutic qualities: massaging, relaxing and soothing one's body; washing away the sweat and grime after a hard day's sightseeing, or (worse still) ten (sometimes stressful) hours behind the wheel of a car. I'm being perfectly serious. Driving in an unfamiliar area, where the traffic is *particularly* heavy, requires not only total concentration, but (as I have said) can be pretty damn stressful.

Yes. My motel room is my home. It's where I sleep, where I put my feet up and watch television (should have put telly, shouldn't I? Never mind). It's where I can write my journal and occasionally (but just occasionally, mind) write postcards, which can then be handed in at the front desk for posting. So simple. And, with coffee making facilities, I can have a brew whenever I wish. Then there is the microwave, in which I can cook, or reheat any of the delights that I may happen upon at the local gas station. The microwave itself (for reasons known only to the motel proprietors) sits graciously atop of the fridge, which, for the most part, serves no purpose whatsoever save to keep me awake at night. Consequently, like a cat being put out for the night, the fridge must be unplugged before I retire to my bed. Finally. Should the neighbours be too noisy for my liking, well then, I can simply ask to be moved to another room, or even another floor.

You know. One of these days, I might just have to write to Stephen Fry, thanking him for this ability I have acquired (simply by reading several of his books) of imagining (from time to time) that I'm *actually* him, when writing some of this nonsense. No offence, Stephen. As they say: *'If a thing works, don't ask how, or why, just be grateful that it does'*. Amen to that.

Again. We come back to therapy. Just as the simple shower, with its soothing jets, *can* have a therapeutic effect, so too can writing, and the simple act of imagining. Don't you agree? Yes. I thought you might.

I had to stop for gas twice yesterday. The first time in Kennebec, where, unfortunately, the gas was $2.75 per gallon. So I gambled and just put $5 worth in, drove about 60 miles down the road to the town of Kimball, where I filled the tank as the gas was a mere $2.61 per gallon. Of course, it doesn't always work that well. Many times in the past, it has been the other way round. But, *'Swings and Roundabouts'*, as they say. *'Swings and Roundabouts.'*

Someone once said that there is a fine line between genius and insanity. There *are* days, when I think that I have a foot in both camps, and days when I have a foot in neither. I'm just drifting helplessly in space. Inwardly, I'm screaming for help, while outwardly, I say nothing. I think the word is, '*Contradiction*'. Am I a contradiction? You know the drill by now: '*Answers on a postcard, and send them to someone who gives a flying fuck*'.

Music. Not much to report. Sadly.

Magical Mystery Tour: The Beatles.

Free Falling: (Now. I really like this song. In fact, it gets better every time I hear it.) Tom Petty and the Heartbreakers.

And finally. The best song she has ever sung, by far.

Crazy for you: Madonna. Or, as I described her in last year's journal: Mad Donna.

Question: When is a bowl of chilli, not a bowl of chilli?

Answer: When it's a cup.

However, a bowl of chilli in one town (or state, for that matter), isn't the same as a bowl of chilli in the next. And no, I'm not just talking about flavour, or taste. For instance. The bowl of chilli I was fortunate enough to be served across the street, just last night, was *three times* larger than other bowls I have been served. '*But was it the best?*' Well no, actually................but it was pretty damn close.

So. A cup is a small serving, while a bowl is a larger serving. Get it? This also applies when ordering soup. Gee! You'll soon know as much as I do.

The chilli was followed by grilled chicken on a bun, with lettuce, tomato, fries and a pickle. Mmmm. I like pickles. They go so well with a burger, don't you find?

Two glasses of Pepsi, and the check came to $14.73. Pricey, for what it was. On the other hand, there was that *extra* large bowl of chilli. So. Score-wise, it has to be 7/10.

10:35am. Check-out is in 25 minutes. So, I'll catch you later.

I've had a lousy fucking day. I've just spent the best part of an hour on the computer in the lobby, composing a long email to Hannah, as, once again, I find myself in a motel where my computer and the outgoing server are not on fucking speaking terms. *'So what does that matter, if you've just sent an email to Hannah on the computer in the lobby?'* I hear you ask. What's the problem? What's the fucking problem? The problem, as you so quaintly put it, is this: It took me so long to type the damn message out (far longer than on my own machine), that after I'd completed my *Masterpiece* and then pressed send, a message appeared, saying, *'Your time has expired, would you like to re-enter your password?'* Consequently, I have absolutely no idea whether or not the message has been sent. Do *you* know?

I guess I could have stayed and retyped the whole damn message out again, but what if the outcome had been the same? No. I'll leave it a week and, maybe by then, she'll have got in touch with me again.

I *really, really* don't feel like doing any work tonight.

No. I'm sorry. No, I'm not! I must stop saying, *Sorry*. I've done nothing wrong. What have I got to be sorry for?

9:20am. Late. But that's okay.

I've had quite a busy morning, involving phone calls and faxes and faxes and phone calls, between Joplin, Missouri and Dickson, Tennessee. It was all to do with my missing Wyndham Rewards points. So now, armed with the correct information, I can email Wyndhams with all the details and claim what is rightfully mine. *Mine! Mine! It's all mine*! Oops. There's me having a bit of a rant, again.

Now, for those of you awaiting an apology over last night's outburst, let me just say this: *'You'll be waiting a fucking long time'*.

I'm crossing the state line into Kansas, sometime today. It's just a stone's throw from here, so, no rush. I'm going to call in at the Route 66 visitors centre in Baxter Springs, for a chat with a lady I met there only last year. Her name's Carolyn Pendleton and she runs the place. Whilst there (last year), I purchased a few souvenirs and was fortunate enough to meet, *'Dean (Crazy Legs) Walker'*.

I slept really well last night, which was odd, as there was a strange noise coming from the air conditioning unit, even though it was switched off. I woke only once, at around 2:30am and then slept right through until 6:30am.

Although (obviously), I don't like being deaf in one ear, it does have its advantages. Yes. If there are any strange noises (and let's face it, there are *always* strange noises in motels), I simply sleep on my good ear. Job sorted.

Breakfast was *interesting*. I had my usual Raisin Bran followed by two pieces of toasted fruit loaf with jam. Yes. I (and my fellow diners) searched in vain for the butter, but butter was there none. I guess we all felt too embarrassed to enquire as to the wherabouts of the ideal accompaniment to one's toast, so I made do with jam. Not quite the same though, is it? Ah! Now then. Here in America, it's called jelly.

This (I have discovered) is one of the older motels in the Super 8 chain. Having said that, it is in an ideal location for your average sightseeing tourist. Joplin is an old town on Route 66 and, fortunately, is close enough to Interstate 44 to keep the place thriving. The town has a profusion of motels and eateries, however, I am not in the mood to list them all. But. You know the score. All the usual suspects are here: Denny's, Bob Evan's, Perkins, Waffle House, Steak 'n' Shake…………you get the picture.

Oh! Before I forget. Whilst in Sioux City, Iowa, I had dinner at Buzz's Grille, and the motel I stayed at cost me $60.48 for the night.

Here in Joplin, the price of my stay is: $68.08 per night.

I spent $29.35 on gas yesterday, but I'm not a happy bunny. No. It's not the price of the gas so much, as the rate at which the engine is consuming it that concerns me. Even though the oil has been changed, my once 400 plus miles to the tank-full car, is now barely 300 miles to the tank-full. However, I do have a theory about this. When I first took possession of this vehicle (and was still getting 400 plus miles per tank-full), it had over 20,000 miles on the clock, and 23,600 by the time I had the oil changed. But! If, after the oil had been changed, the mileage was still low, then it naturally follows that the age of the engine (mileage-wise) must come into play here. You see, I've never had a rental car (in the past) that has had *anywhere near* that amount of miles on the clock. I'll leave it a couple of days, then phone Avis again and see if I can change this *Gas-guzzling, gas-aholic*. I swear, it can drink more gas than I used to drink beer, and that's a lot.

10:30am. I'm well behind on my writing, but I haven't time to do any more right now. Must catch up this evening.

3:40pm. I left Joplin at 10:55am. Where am I now? I'm in the little town of Baxter Springs, Kansas. Which is…about…I would say…approximately…25 miles from Joplin. Yes folks. That's right. You heard me. 25 miles.

Turning left out of the motel (Super 8) I headed north on Highway 71 for several miles, before heading west on 7th Street, which is part of the old alignment (Route 66). After driving for several more miles, I crossed the state line from Missouri into Kansas and found myself in the tiny town of Galena, a town I visited only last year.

Once again, I'm getting ahead of myself. But that's what happens when you don't stay on top of your writing.

One might argue that, with so much of one's time taken up with writing, when on earth does one have the time to enjoy oneself? Of course, my argument would be that without the writing I run the risk of going *completely* round the bend (insane).

Although, to an extent, I *do* enjoy my road trips, they are, let's face it, a mere facet of life. As you know, I am no great lover of life, therefore I can never fully enjoy them (not 100 per cent). I'd stick my head in the oven now, if I were you.

The weather conditions yesterday were atrocious. It rained continually. All the way from Sioux City, Iowa, right down to Joplin, Missouri. In fact, going through Kansas City on the interstate, the rain was so heavy that although the speed limit was 65mph (which usually means that the traffic is doing at least 75mph), the fastest vehicles (myself included) were only doing 45mph. Now that tells you something, doesn't it?

Coming through east Omaha (although Omaha is in Nebraska, the eastern edge of it is in Iowa) I encountered no problems negotiating the interstates. I was on Interstate 29, which became the 29/80 for a short time, but then switched back to the 29. However, whilst negotiating the 435 (which skirts around the edge of Kansas City), due to the heavy rain and even heavier traffic, I missed the turn off for Highway 71. But, it was simply a case of driving up to the next exit, turning around and coming back. A mere five minutes, that's all. So what? There was no shortage of roadworks on that section of the highway, so I was forced to go slow anyway.

Ah! Now then. Before I forget. After the fiasco on the computer in the lobby, I got back to my room and, as you know, I was more than a little upset. But, after having my rant, I remembered something that the Native American Indian I was fortunate enough to meet in Rapid City had told me. So, I looked at the scribbled notes I had made whilst he was explaining the mysteries of the computer to me, and I thought to myself, '*What if I......no......couldn't possibly be right......but......maybe...... oh, sod it. Just follow the instructions, as you've written them*'. So, I ignored my usual method of going straight to my emails and opted instead for the Internet. And, lo and behold, there was an email button. I pressed the button and up pops another screen, where I simply entered my user name (email address) and password (................) (Never you mind. It's none of your damn business) and Bob's your uncle, and Fanny's your aunt, and the birds are singing, and it's a hap, hap, happy day and whatever you've got to do........blah, blah, blah.

Was I happy, or was I happy? I was so happy (not to mention proud of myself) I could have, could have......Well. I could have done something......had I been able to think of *anything* to do.

Yes. So there it was. I felt like Steve McQueen in '*The Great Escape*'. I could see the Swiss border. I could smell freedom. Finally, it was within my grasp.

A whole new email page was right there in front of me, beckoning me, welcoming me, like a free gift waiting to be snapped up. What could possibly go wrong?

To whom it may concern.

The author (regrettable though it may seem), has charged *me* with the task of informing *you* (and by *you*, I mean the reader), that as he no longer has any interest in completing this journal, he *suggests* that you simply finish it yourself.

Thank you. And, goodnight.

THE END

Ha! Gotcha!

Damn. Where was I up to?

Ah, yes. Emails.

I typed as fast as I could, all the time thinking that I was still on the computer in the lobby, and up against the clock. But which clock? It didn't say (when I started typing) that I had only a limited amount of time in which to write, and then send my email. But that didn't matter anymore. I was on my own machine now, and the only possible obstacle (as far as I could see), would be whether or not my email could be sent. But then, why wouldn't it? Unlike my usual email section, which as a rule I normally have no problem with, this section, the Internet section, had no yellow triangle with a black exclamation mark on it. Hey! Why doesn't it go the whole hog and display a skull and cross bones in a neon sign? Yeah! See if I care.

So there I was, my finger hovering over the button, like some demented president who desperately wants to know, *'I wonder what would really happen, if I were to push this?'* while the cursor sat impatiently atop the send button, saying: *'Come on, come on. This is getting scary'*. So, I pressed the button and what do you suppose happened? Yes. Like a genie in a puff of smoke, the message was gone, and in its place were the words: *'Your Message Has Been Sent'*. Eureka!

Of course, the irony here is that I am still receiving emails, but they don't arrive at the Internet email section, they still go to the other section. Still. Who cares?

Yes. I think we've covered all the bases. Ah! No. There's just yesterday's music. And we all love a bit of music, don't we?

Evil Woman: (the less said on that subject, the better) E. L. O.

Money for nothing: Dire Straits.

Spirit in the sky: Medicine Head (I think). Hm. Might have been Doctor and the Medics. Who knows?

Benny and the Jets: Elton John.

You can't hurry love: Phil Collins (originally done by Diana Ross).

And last, but not least, my favourite song.

Woman: John Lennon.

6:30pm. I've only got the day's events to do. But, before that, I need an FVC.

Later, folks. Hey! Where's the nearest gas station?

7:20pm. Not bad. Just a two mile round trip. $1.28 for a large coffee, and $1 for a paper.

Okay. So where were we?

As I headed along 7th Street, in Joplin, I saw a sign at a carwash that read: $3 Carwash. Yeah. Right. So what do they do? Wave a wet shammy leather in front of your vehicle and say, *'Hey! Don't you feel cleaner, now?'*

Further along, but just off 7th Street, I caught a glimpse of the Facet Sound Recording Studio, and it put me in mind of the time I visited the Sun Studios in Memphis.

Sam Phillips ran the studio, and it was he who gave Elvis (and later Johnny Cash) his big break (as they say in the world of show business). But what year was that? Was it 1955? Might even have been the year before. I'm pretty sure that Johnny Cash got his big break in 1957, though I could be wrong.

Yes, that really was something special. Standing in the same studio where Elvis had stood all those years earlier, holding the very same microphone that he had held and having my picture taken. Now, if I remember rightly, that would have been 2005. My only regret is that it wasn't a microphone that Lennon had held. *'C'est la vie'*.

Another mile or so down the road I passed a fairground. Just a small one. I remember thinking how out of place it looked, on this main highway. Still. Maybe there was a large car park behind it. And maybe it was a big attraction in the summer. Who knows?

The road was unfamiliar, even though I'd driven down it only the year before. I guess back then I was concentrating on the road so much (and trying hard not to make any mistakes), that I simply didn't see any of what was to my right or left.

West of Joplin, the road (the old road) got rough, and even rougher as I crossed the state line into Kansas, and the little town of Galena, which, because of the weather conditions (wild and windy), looked even more ghostly than it had the year before, when it was blue skies and sunshine, all the way.

Four Women On The Route, the store I stopped at last year to buy a few souvenirs, was closed. I guess with all the bad weather they'd been having in America, they just haven't seen enough tourists around that way to make it worth while opening up the store. Of course, there are always idiots like me, who turn up when you least expect them to.

However, I was more upset when I reached the Route 66 visitors centre, in Baxter Springs, only to find that it too was closed. I was so looking forward to having a chat with Carolyn. (Carolyn Pendleton is the director of that fine establishment.)

Between Galena and Baxter Springs, you'll find Riverton. Unlike the previous year, I had a little drive around. Apart from a high school, a bank and a Conoco gas station, there was nothing except for houses, dwellings, abodes, or whatever you want to call them. Nothing of any interest. Well. Not to me.

Last year, whilst chatting to one of the ladies in Four Women On The Route, she told me that they had plans to develop the building directly across the street from them (which wasn't in that bad a state of repair) and the *really* dilapidated place over to their right, which, long ago (when Galena *was* somewhere) had been a brothel, among other things.

It breaks my heart when I drive through towns like Galena. Yet, I am drawn back to them, time and time again. Why? Am *I* stuck in the past?

Though small, Baxter Springs has a pretty impressive museum. I would most certainly recommend that you visit the place, if you should find yourself out this way.

Baxter Springs Museum. 740 East Ave, Baxter Springs, Kansas. 66713. http:/home.4state.com/~heritagectr

Check it out.

8:55pm. Now, before I rest my weary typing finger and before I give you what little there was in the way of music today, I must tell you that I am not staying at one of my usual establishments, where I am able collect my Wyndham Rewards points. Neither am I staying at the Baxter Springs Motel, which is where I stayed last year. Oh no. But, you are going to have to wait until the morning to find out where I spent this evening. Ah! The plot thickens.

Music.

Glory Days: (great song) Bruce Springsteen.

Miss you: The Rolling Stones.

Sorry folks, that's all we've got for tonight. But hey! Why not join me tomorrow? We can do a little road trip together. How about it?

9:15am. Something's just occurred to me. Whilst still in Joplin (on Thursday night) I ate dinner at Denny's. You remember Denny's, don't you? It was, for quite some time, a chain I regularly patronized. However, on my last couple of visits (in different states) I've noticed that the menus have gotten smaller (or is that just my imagination?) and the food just hasn't been *nearly* as good as I remembered it. But, I'd had a long (not to mention *difficult)* drive through the torrential rain and, as I really didn't feel like venturing too far afield, I decided (reluctantly) to settle for Denny's, which was just next door to the motel.

I ordered the deep-fried shrimp, Tilapia with avocado salsa and mashed potato. The shrimps came with a spicy tomato dip and the Tilapia was not over-seasoned (as was the case in Red Lobster). It was, however, nowhere near as tasty. The avocado salsa was quite pleasant. I can't remember the last time I ate avocado. Probably ten years, or more. Then there was the mashed potato. Ah! It was like nothing I'd ever seen before. The colour was yellow, and it contained onions and small pieces of spicy sausage. (Pepperoni? Who knows?) And, with an apple and mango soda, the bill came to $14.40. I left a $3 tip. And as for marks out of ten, it has to be a 6. Oh, Denny's. Whatever happened to you?

Baxter Springs.

After leaving the museum (a little after 2:00pm) I decided that, as I wouldn't be doing much more driving that day (yesterday), I'd have a spot of lunch for a change. As a rule, I don't eat lunch while on holiday. Well, I'm always on the move. I don't have time to stop for lunch.

But, *'a change is as good as a rest'*, as they say. So, I headed for the *Café on the Route*, as recommended by a very pleasant young lady at the museum.

The *Café on the Route* is part of *The Little Brick Inn*, which is also a bed and breakfast. (Which, incidentally, is where I've just eaten. But more of that later.)

The property was once the Crowell Bank Building, and is reputed to have been robbed by none other than Jesse James and Cole Younger.

Though they have an extensive menu, I opted for one of the day's specials, as recommended by the waitress. I plumped for the cheese, ham and spinach soup, followed by the tender brisket in barbecue sauce, with wild rice salad and a bread roll. And, with a glass of coke, the bill *would* have been less than $8, but I can't be any more specific, as it was added to the price of my room. So how do I know that the bill would have been no more than $8, if I did not pay there and then? Simple. I'd already been given the bill before I'd decided to stay the night and, as it came to a mere $7 before tax, I think I can safely say that even if it *had* come to more than $8, it wouldn't have been much more. So there.

The Café (or restaurant) is located on the ground floor (though in America, it's the first floor), whilst up stairs, there are (at present) seven bedrooms, one of which (mine, obviously) I shall describe in detail later.

Lunch, my room and breakfast, came to a mere $78.92. Now that's a bargain.

And, for those of you who like to surf the net (as they say), here are a couple of websites for you:

Thelittlebrickinn.com

Cafeontheroute.com

This establishment is run by Richard & Amy Sanell, and is located at: 1101 Military Avenue, Baxter Springs, Kansas, 66713. U S A.

There. That's made your day, hasn't it?

I didn't bother with dinner. Well, I had that large lunch, you see.

After lunch, I checked in, got my gear out of the car and made the long trip up the stairs to my room. The staircase was unusually wide, as befits a building of this standing (a former bank) and had no carpet. No. It was just dark, varnished wood, every step of which creaked as I ascended. The hallway on that upper floor was, like the staircase, dark varnished wood.

As I struggled with my cases up this fine, old staircase, it put me in mind of one of those old black and white movies from the forties or fifties.

You'd see a man (or woman) walk up the stairs, along the corridor and then tap lightly on the door of a private eye, or an attorney. A voice from behind the closed door would simply say: *'Yeah.'* A gloved hand would turn the door handle, the door would open ever so slowly and in would step a sultry looking blonde, with an hourglass figure, a skirt so tight that she probably had to put it on with a shoehorn, a thrusting cleavage that doubled as a bottle opener, six inch stiletto heels, which supported legs that went all the way to heaven and pouting lips with gold medal winning potential. Oh yes. They always had pouting lips. As she entered the smoke- filled room, she'd encounter a rather slovenly looking character (though handsome with it), who'd be leaning back in his chair, still wearing his fedora, cigarette hanging out of the corner of his mouth and with his feet on the desk. He'd say: *'Something I can do for you, Blondie?'* She'd reply: *'Yeah. Matter of fact, there is.'*

Oh. You get the picture.

10:45am. I'll be back in a minute. Just got to find out what time check-out is.

5:05pm. I'm afraid to say that I'm not at all happy.

You see, I've just spent the last 45 minutes or so, composing an email to my sister, only to be told by the fucking computer that I was out of time and that I should start again. This also happened to me whilst using the computer in the lobby at the Super 8 motel, in Joplin. But tell me this, if you can. When sending an email via the Internet, how long do you have to compose it? Nowhere on the screen does it say: *'You have X amount of minutes to compose and then send your email'.*

So where was I?

There were 24 steps up to the landing. That's an awful lot when you're carrying a suitcase, *and* a shoulder bag.

I've lost interest in imagining the place in its heyday. Perhaps I'll let my imagination off the leash when I'm feeling a little more upbeat.

How would I describe the colour of the walls in my room. (Yes. Although I am at present residing in a very comfortable suite at a Super 8 motel in Perry, Oklahoma, I am still talking about the *Little Brick Inn*.) Phew. Glad we got that sorted out. It's bad enough that I'm so confused, without you keep asking me, *'Are we there yet? Can we stop for ice cream?'* and, *'I need to go to the toilet.'* Oh, shut up.

When a colour (any colour) becomes as pale as it can be, it's practically impossible to differentiate between any of the colours of the spectrum. So. Were the walls really, really pale yellow? Or, were they really, really pale green? Damned if I know. I don't even think I care. I did last night, but I'm upset now, so I don't really give a toss.

The floors in both the bathroom and the bedroom had been sanded and varnished, just like the stairs and hallway.

The room was large, with a high ceiling and an interesting mishmash of furniture.

Next to the bed was a reasonably sized wicker table, on which sat a digital alarm clock, a table lamp, a Bible and a diary. *'But why a diary?'* I hear you ask. Simple. So those who stay in the room, can, not only write a review of the establishment, but also, read the comments of others. Neat, eh?

Another wicker table had been placed against the wall, close to the door and between two chairs (one easy chair and one wicker chair). The latter had been painted white. Oh! And the easy chair was green, and very comfortable.

On top of the second wicker table sat a wicker basket filled with artificial flowers, while underneath, two pretty ancient looking books had been strategically placed to arouse the interest of the occupant, no doubt. (They didn't arouse my interest. Well, not enough to open them.)

Next to the white wicker chair, which was in a corner of the room, was an upright metal cabinet which had been painted a blue-grey colour and was the kind of thing one might expect to find in a workshop. On the shelves of its pink interior, were a selection of books, a rag doll and a few ornaments.

At the foot of the bed sat yet another (this time wooden) table, supporting another wicker basket containing artificial leaves.

Between the easy chair and the wicker table was a free-standing reading lamp, whilst on the wall, just above the wicker table, could be found a picture depicting a rural scene.

I'll bet you're bloody glad you tuned in for this, aren't you folks? Oh, shut up. I'm on a roll.

The ceiling supported a propeller fan, with four lamps connected to it. The bloody thing switched itself on while I was out getting a coffee. Damn cheek.

In the corner, adjacent to the wicker chair, a metal frame with clothes rail and hangers was attached to the wall.

Directly opposite the bed was a curiously interesting piece of nondescript furniture (if that makes any sense. Though I can assure you, if you saw it, you'd understand) that supported the television.

The bed, though comfortable, was creaky. (I liked that.) The headboard, made of both wood and fabric, was pale blue and had a well worn look to it.

There were no curtains. Just horizontal blinds.

Beneath the clothes rack, there was a foldaway device on which to balance one's suitcase.

The bathroom, though clean, did not have a plug in the sink, which *could* have made shaving just a little tricky the following morning, but I had a plan.

All in all, it was quite a pleasant room, really.

When asked (yesterday) what time I would be requiring breakfast, I replied, *"About eight, if that's alright."* Sure enough, at eight on the dot, there was a knock on the door, and a voice just said, *"Mr O'Leary",* in an enquiring way, and that was it. I didn't need to answer the door, I simply left my room, walked to the dining area (which was upstairs), where waiting just for me was a plate of eggs, sausage burgers, two *very* large pancakes with butter and maple syrup, a plate of fresh fruit (water melon, strawberry and kiwi fruit), a large glass of orange juice and half a pot of coffee. Can you guess what I did? Yes. Of course you can. I scoffed the bloody lot. You can't beat a good breakfast.

After checking out, I was at a bit of a loss as to what to do. So, I headed back to Galena, in the hope of finding the 'Four Women On The Route' open this time. Sadly, it was not.

The weather, for a change, was beautiful. The sun was shining, there was not a cloud in the sky and the wind had dropped.

I wandered aroud the area for a while, took several photos and then decided it was time to get the hell out of Dodge. Okay! So I've seen a lot of Westerns. It's not a crime, is it?

I took the short drive back to Baxter Springs, got onto Highway 166 and drove about 160 miles across the south eastern part of Kansas, before joining Interstate 35 and then drove south for about 60 miles, before deciding I'd had enough for one day.

So, here I am in Perry. I've no idea exactly where the town is (location-wise, that is), or how many occupants it has. All I know for sure is that I can see the interstate. Right now, that's all I care about. When I'm not feeling very happy (and let's face it, I've had better days), it's comforting to know, that I can always hit the highway. Like a tornado, I can be here one minute and gone the next.

I've just had dinner at Braum's. I guess you could call it a fast food joint. But hey! I've had some pretty crummy meals at supposedly decent diners and restaurants, just lately. So. I'm pleased to report, that the meal wasn't half bad.

Braum's seems to specialize in a variety of burgers (well, what self respecting fast food joint doesn't?), ice cream and milk shakes. But, it does far more than that. A relatively large section of it is like a mini-mart. Yeah! They sell all kinds of good stuff, even fruit and veg. So. Here's *one* fast food joint, that is actually going up in the world.

Having not eaten since breakfast, I have to say, I was more than a little peckish. *'Mmmmm. Chilli.'* Damn! It's that Homer Simpson guy again.

Yes. You guessed it. I ordered the chilli, which was topped with peppers, onions, grated cheese and sour cream. If you never had sour cream with your chilli, then I suggest you give it a try. Oh! And a bowl of chilli just wouldn't be complete without those crackers that you crumble while they are still in the packet, and then mix in with that culinary delight.

After my chilli (which, by the way, was delicious), I had absolutely no problem whatsoever polishing off grilled chicken in a bun with salad, a large portion of fries and a large soda. All this yummy food could have been yours (if you were here), for the outrageously low price of $11.11. All the ones: One-ty-one. Now you know why I'm not a Bingo caller.

What time is it? Ah! 8:20pm. Good. All I've got to do now is give you the day's music, and I'm free. Yep. Looks like an early finish for a change.

A day in the life: The Beatles.

Here I go again: (what a fantastic song that is) White Snake.

Take me home: Phil Collins.

Give a little bit: Supertramp.

Yep. You'll certainly get a welcome in Galena, Kansas.

Four Women on the Route (66) Gift Shop and Café. Galena, Kansas.

Route 66 Visitors Centre. Baxter Springs, Kansas.

Sunday November 1st

8:30am.

Eureka! Eu-Flaming-Reka!

All I wanted to know, was how long my sessions lasted once I got onto the web to send my emails. Because, as you know ('cos I told you so), I can no longer go through the normal channels when sending emails anymore, due to the lack of communication between the outgoing server and my machine.

So why am I now so happy? Well, that would be because I now know that my sessions (when sending emails via the Internet) are a mere 15 minutes. Yes. If after logging on, I have not composed and sent my email, my session will be over and I will have to sign in again. What's worse is that if you should go over, there is no warning, no message that says: *'you have 30 seconds to complete this task'*. Nothing. You can spend an hour, two hours, three hours, how ever long you like, but *then*, ah, yes, *then*, when you press the send button, it has the audacity to tell you that you are out of time. Try again. *'BASTARD!'*

And what could be worse than this? I shall tell you. It doesn't even have the decency to save all the work you've already put in. *'DOUBLE BASTARD!'*

Last night, I spent the best part of 45 minutes, composing a really lovely email to my sister, Judith, only for the evil beast to refuse to send my message. At least now I know why.

15 minutes. 15 bloody minutes. I ask you. What way is this to run a company? I'll tell you this. If I didn't enjoy being on the road so much, I'd spend the rest of my holiday back in Rapid City. I didn't have any problems with the outgoing server there. Oh no.

By my calculations, it should be about 160 miles to Hinton. (A town 30 miles east of Clinton.) I'm sure I've told you about the town of Clinton, haven't I? Well, it was where I had the worst steak in my life, and believe me, I've eaten an awful lot of steak over here. Now why do we use the word 'awful' in a sentence?

It seems to suggest that something is unpleasant, yet it isn't. *The weather was awful.* Now that makes sense. But. *We had an awfully good time.* Seems so illogical, does it not? Bah! Humbug! I'll never understand this English language. It's all Greek to me. *'What? That makes absolutely no sense whatsoever.'* Yeah. Precisely. That's what I've been saying all along.

Did I not just tell you that?

I think I told you that.

Yes, I did tell you that.

Anyway. It was the year of the great depression. No. Wait a minute. Hang on a *mo.* It was the year of *my* great depression. Here we go again. *'Illogicality.'* How can one be on one's holidays (and in theory, enjoying oneself), yet still get depressed? Ah! Well. Now then. We're treading on dangerous ground here. Though depression may *appear* to be illogical, it is, nevertheless, as lethal as the deadliest poison known to man, of that I can assure you. For the sufferer has to spend his (or her) entire life constantly monitoring the condition, just as the diabetic monitors his insulin levels. Believe me when I tell you, it's not easy.

Enough of that, for now. I may well return to it at some later stage, should the mood take me. Sometimes, just talking about it can be quite therapeutic.

Piccante Grill, Clinton, Oklahoma. I've never had a steak like it. Even a dog would have struggled to eat that. I'm not joking when I say that you could have used it to re-sole your shoe. I had a couple of bites, and that was it.

Whenever I'm around this way, I always pop into the Route 66 museum, just to see if they've got any new souvenirs, something to add to my collection of Route 66 memorabilia.

However, I thought I'd stop at the town of Hinton as, (a) I've never been there before and it's always nice to visit new towns, even though I don't often get to see that much of them, and, (b) I thought I'd check out another one of those Microtels. The last one I stayed at was on Moxie lane, in Delphos, Ohio, if you remember. That was the place where I had dinner at that bar, and you thought I'd had a drink. Now, don't lie. You did! You know you did.

5:30pm. No. Wasn't too impressed with Hinton. Well, when I say I wasn't too impressed, I don't mean with the town (not that I saw the town), or the motel. No. It was that ruddy great truck stop next to the motel, and the fact that it was far too close to the interstate. Too noisy, on both counts.

I hadn't wanted to stay in Clinton, but in Clinton, here I am.

I'm staying at a Days Inn Motel (my second of this trip, to be precise) and, at $68.70 per night, I'd say it was a bargain. Although they *do* have a restaurant here, unfortunately, it is closed on a Sunday. But wait! What's that? It's another eatery. Now what's does that sign say? I can't quite make it out. *'The Piccante Grill?' Noooooooo!*

Fortunately, when chatting to the young lady at reception (recounting the tale of my leather steak) she gave me directions to a little Mexican place that serves good food. She too, had eaten at Piccante Grill, and had not been at all impressed with it.

Speaking of food, it's 5:55pm. Time for tea.

7:25pm.

'El Cid'. Now *there's* a name.

Yes. This was where I had dinner. Or should I say, *'Tea'*.

The place was small. Although my meal was nothing to write home about, it was far better than the last meal I ate (tried to eat) in this town.

With a very simple interior, you could say that, *'what you see is what you get'*, with *El Cid*. The atmosphere was not what one would call warming, though the waitress was polite and friendly.

The walls of the interior were a strange mix of orange and lime green. Curious. In the corner, the television was on a Spanish channel, showing Mexican football and was being viewed by an appreciative audience of three. Yes. That included me.

Though it is only November 1ˢᵗ, Christmas decorations already adorned the walls.

The menu was a mystery to me. Oh sure, I could read the words, chicken, beef and pork, but what did the Spanish words mean? How was the beef, chicken and pork to be cooked? And what would it be served with? I looked at the beautiful young waitress, held up my hands and said, *" I'm sorry, but I don't understand. The only word I recognize, is 'Tacos'."* She smiled sympathetically, though probably thought me a complete idiot.

As with most Mexican restaurants, whilst waiting for my meal, I was presented with a large basket of tortillas, accompanied by a hot chilli sauce.

The three Tacos, containing shredded beef and fresh coriander (at least, I think it was coriander), were served with rice and a kind of a bean stew, topped with grated cheese. The meal also came with three wedges of lime, though I had no idea why. So, I opened each taco, and squeezed the lime juice over them. Interesting.

I have to admit, that after studying the menu for several minutes and realizing that I was out of my depth, I was sorely tempted (when the waitress came back) to say, *'Oh, I'll just have what he's having over there'.* Then, she really would have thought me a complete idiot.

I ordered a coke with my meal. This came with neither straw, nor glass and was in the tallest, slimmest coke bottle I'd ever seen.

Would I eat there again? Well......probably. But next time, I definitely will say, *'I'll just have what he's having, and don't spare the horses'.*

The bill was $9.75, and I left $2 for the pretty lady. Well. She deserved it, for having to put up with an idiot like me.

After leaving Perry....No! No! No! Perry's not a *person.* Perry is the name of the town in which I spent last night. Oh, I do wish you'd keep up.

It's approximately 60 miles from Perry to Oklahoma City (heading south on Interstate 35) and all the way, I was in two minds as to whether I should head west in the direction of Texas, or east back to Tennessee to change this damn car. Yes. I'm still concerned about the mileage I'm getting. (Or should that be, not getting?) As I got into the city, I saw a sign that read, *'Visitors Information Centre'*. (You'll notice that I've spelt 'Centre' with an RE, even though I'm in America, where it is spelt the other way round. And the reason for this? Because I don't imagine that anyone from America will ever get to read this stuff.) I decided to stop at the centre and use their pay phone. Sadly, although they used to have a phone, it had been taken out.

Whilst there (I do love the word, *Whilst*. It's so much better than *While*.), I got chatting to a lady who works at the centre, and apart from trying to sort out the world's problems, which, let's face it, is a mammoth task for two people, we also talked about cars and gas. She informed me that this new eco-friendly fuel they have in America (containing 10% ethanol) gives far less miles to the gallon than the regular unleaded. Eco-friendly? Maybe. Financially friendly? Absolutely not.

I purchased several Route 66 badges, and decided that it wasn't worth all the bother taking the car back to Nashville. So, I filled the tank in the gas station across the street from the centre, and headed west.

Yep. I'm really glad that I stopped in at the visitors centre, as it put my mind at rest. There obviously isn't anything wrong with the engine, it's just the gas. Anyway. We'll see what happens next year.

On the outskirts of Oklahoma City is the little town of Yukon, a place where, back in 2004, I had spent the night at a Super 8 Motel. Oddly enough, I scanned a photograph of that very motel into my computer several months ago, but I couldn't for the life of me remember where it was. I knew that the motel had been somewhere *in* Oklahoma, so that's all I wrote on my computer: *'A motel in Oklahoma'*. Well. There's another mystery solved.

I drove through old Yukon and on into El Reno, which, incidentally, is a town I stayed in only last year. Now what was the name of that diner I ate at? Damn! Can't remember. Anyway, it's in last year's journal. Wait a minute! Wasn't it, *'J & Kay's Restaurant'?* Yes. That seems to ring a bell.

I got lost in El Reno, and overshot the runway in Fort Reno. But, you know the score. I just headed up to the next exit, turned around and headed back-a-ways.

I spent a very pleasant hour talking to the couple who run the Fort Reno Visitors Centre. But more of that tomorrow. It's 9:20pm. I'm so damn tired. And, as they say in theatrical circles: *'Always leave them wanting more'.* Goodnight.

9:10am. Well that was a bit of a let-down, I must say.

I showered, shaved, brushed my teeth, got dressed and headed off to reception, in search of my free breakfast, only to discover that the only thing that was free was the coffee. Oh, bother! Yes. I am showing a little restraint.

Fortunately (or, unfortunately, if you happen to object to paying for breakfast, as I do, in these *slightly* more expensive motels), the *'Branding Iron Restaurant'* (which is attached to the motel) was open for business, so, I took advantage of this fact and stuffed my face, with a ham, bacon and sausage omelette, generously topped with grated cheese. The omelette was served with hash browns, toast and all the coffee I could drink. And the bill? $8.75 plus a $2 tip. Good food. I'll grant you that. But, I've gotten out of the habit of forking out for breakfast every morning. Still. It *did* make a pleasant change from Raisin Bran. *'Raisin Bran'*. If I eat much more of that stuff, I'll start looking like a packet.

Ah, good! I just checked the back of the door (where they have all the relevant information), and fortunately, checkout is not until 12 noon, which is just as well, as I'm running a little late. Yes. That's right. It's happened. I have now reached the point where (I'm glad to say) I'm actually sleeping normally. Not that I really understand what a normal night's sleep is.

It's so annoying. I could have kept writing last night, even though I was more than a little tired, and at least I would have had the day's events typed up. However, I thought I'd watch the box for a while, before hitting the hay, as it were.

Now, I don't know if you know this, but I do enjoy forensic programmes and shows about real life crimes and how they are solved, which is why I ended up watching the telly until after midnight.

Fort Reno. Well, as the name suggest, it was the site of an old fort. Unfortunately, I can impart no more information on the subject, as I spent the entire time talking to the wonderful married couple who ran the place. Although I was given a couple of leaflets, to date, I have read neither of them. Having said that, I do know that, apart from the visitors centre (which houses a small museum containing various military artefacts) on the site, you will also find both a chapel and a cemetery. And! The lady at the centre reliably informed me that, she *had* seen a ghost (in military uniform) disappearing through a wall, on more than one occasion. You can make of that what you will, but I believe her.

Had I stayed in the town of Hinton, I would most certainly have visited Red Rock Canyon, as was recommended by the couple at the centre. I'm sorry that I have to keep referring to them as *'the couple'*, but I didn't think to ask their names.

On so many occasions, whilst on my travels, I've found myself chatting to people, (sometimes for hours) and although I shall always remember their faces, I haven't a clue what their names are.

That's road tripping for you. It not an easy job. But let's face it, *'someone's gotta do it'*. And that someone might as well be me.

Last night's music. No. *Yesterday's* music.

In too deep: (beautiful song) Phil Collins.

Won't get fooled again: The (inimitable) Who. Ah! Now then. The theme tune to CSI Miami.

Cold as ice: Foreigner. Now, when was the last time you heard that?

10:20am. I'll leave at around 11:00am.

It's about 250 miles to Amarillo, which should, if I'm lucky, be a four hour drive. However, I must first stop at the Route 66 museum here in Clinton and see what's on offer. I think I'll buy the revised edition of the EZ66 guide, by Jerry McClanahan. My old one was printed in 2005, but these days there's always something new happening along the old route. Hey! I like that. *'Always something new happening along the old route'*. Cool, man.

5:10pm. I'm back in Amarillo, and although I was planning on staying at a cheaper motel, this one (another Super 8) is reasonably priced at $58.56.

I haven't got long. Oh, no! Am I starting to sound like Tony Hancock again? No. What I mean is, I've not got long before dinner. Oh! How I wish I could make up my mind. *Dinner? Tea? 'Could you not use one or the other?'*

Now. I *would* like to offer you an apology, unfortunately, I'm fresh out. Though, if you'd care to wait, I *am* expecting a delivery any day now.

No. This is no good. I just haven't got the enthusiasm to write at the moment. I'll try again later.

7:45pm. Yep. It's later, alright. But do I now feel like writing? Nope. But, I've got to get it done. I'd only be upset with myself if I missed a day or two. In fact, if I *did* miss a day's writing, it might depress me so much, that I could quite easily delete the whole fucking lot and then where would I be? Yes! Quite! You're not wrong there. I'd be up the Swanee without a paddle.

The Big Texan.

I first visited the place only last year. What a place! Quite magnificent. I did write about my experience in last year's journal, so I won't bore you with *those* details again.

My motel is located on Frontage Road, on the north side of the interstate and just off exit 72a. So, to get to the Big Texan, I must first turn right as I leave the motel and head up to the junction, go left under the interstate, left again onto South Frontage Road, get onto the slip road, take the interstate down to exit 75, do a U-turn under the interstate, back onto North Frontage Road and then it's just a short way down on the right. (The Big Texan.)

'Hm. Interesting. So why don't you just make a left out of the motel, and drive straight down North Frontage Road, thus taking a more direct route?' I hear you ask. The answer is simple. In fact, I'm sure the more intelligent among you have already worked it out. Frontage Road North, and Frontage Road South are both

one way. The north runs east to west, while the south runs west to east.

As I sat there, admiring all the steers' heads (complete with horns), the cow hides and all the other Western paraphernalia, Big John Henry was up on the stage, anticipating the *ultimate*. Yes. John Henry, a big black guy from God knows where, was about to tackle 72 ounces of prime Texas beef, a baked potato, a shrimp cocktail and a bread roll, and all in one hour. Man, that's crazy.

As the plates of food were put down in front of him, a large group of diners crowded around and took photographs. As the clock went down to 59 minutes and 59 seconds, Big John Henry got stuck in.

But! Do you know what really annoyed me about it all? It was the fact that the battery in my *new* camera was low and wouldn't allow me to take any pictures. Oh, Gawd. I feel a Victor Meldrew moment coming on.

And *my* meal? Oh, I think you're going to love this.

I opted for the, '*Six Flags of Texas*'. I guess you *could* call it a combo meal. For it consisted of, two large chicken strips, four large catfish fillets, three large shrimps and four large spare ribs. This little lot (little lot?) came with two sauces: tartare sauce for the shrimp and catfish, and a spicy tomato sauce for the chicken. The ribs were quite happily swimming in their own barbecue sauce and had absolutely no intention of sharing it with either the chicken, or the fish.

Accompaniments: Texas rice. A little salty, but not bad. A plate of vegetables, which included: cauliflower, broccoli, carrots and baby onions. And, with two bread rolls and three glasses of Pepsi, I was as happy as a pig in.........in.........in.........in The Big Texan.

When I first sat down and looked at the menu, my eyes went straight to the steak. No! Not *that* steak. While it's true that when on my holidays, I can eat considerably more than when I'm at home, I would never be so stupid as to attempt such a gargantuan feat. Not that I'm saying that John Henry and all the others are stupid, it's just that I wouldn't have a hope in hell of eating even half that amount. No. My eyes focused on the advert that said: *'Our 50ᵗʰ Anniversary Steak. A tribute to man versus food. 18 ounce sirloin (¼ of 72 ounce) 3 shrimps, baked potato, salad and a bread roll. And all for $20.10.'* And have you any idea what that is in pound sterling? It's about £12.60. It would cost the best part of that for that amount of steak in the supermarket, back home.

It wasn't that I couldn't have eaten that amount of steak, it's just that I've eaten so much steak on this trip already, I thought I'd try something different.

My meal (including tax) came to $24.53. Including a tip, it cost me $28. Now if that's not a bargain, then I don't know what is.

As for a mark. Well, the food was good, though not the best I'd eaten. All the same, I think I can just about stretch to an 8/10. Bravo.

Yeah. The Big Texan, man. Give it a try sometime.

About 8 miles west of Clinton, I left the interstate at exit 57 and got onto the old road. You see, I'd got the distance wrong. It's not 250 miles from Clinton to Amarillo, it's a mere 172miles. So, as I had more time than I had originally thought, I decided upon a leisurely drive along Route 66, rather than a race down the interstate.

It was soul destroying, going through the little town of Canute. People still live in the town, of course, but the devastation that one sees in towns like Canute, since the building of the interstates (albeit, many years ago now), to me at least, is obscene. Though my eyes see only the devastation that is, my mind sees the beauty that was.

I stopped for gas in a town called Erick, just 7 miles from the Texas line. I still had half a tank full, but, as I needed a leak, I thought I may as well stick $10 worth in the tank. Shortly after leaving Erick…… No! Don't start with the silly jokes again. You know full well that Erick is the name of a town. Can we get on? Now where was I? You made me lose my place. Okay. So, shortly after leaving Erick, a car overtook me, and the licence plate read: Divine 1. Just at that moment, there was a religious song on the radio, and the words the guy was singing (at that very moment) were: *'Blessed be the name of the Lord.'* Now, what are the odds of that?

I took Route 66 into Texas as far as Shamrock, a town I stayed in only last year. I stopped in at the U-Drop Inn, one section of which houses the Chamber of Commerce. Like so many of the buildings on the old road, with the advent of the interstates, this fine old Art Deco building (dating back to 1936), that had been a Conoco gas station and a diner, quickly fell into a state of disrepair. Fortunately, the building has now been restored to its former glory, and I would strongly advise that you pay it a visit the next time you're up this way. Listen! Don't just think about it. *Do it!* Before it's too late.

If, when I die, I can come back to earth (as a spirit, of course, for that is the only way I would ever return to *this* planet) I would choose to be a ghostly figure, in a ghostly Chevy, who is regularly seen cruising up and down the old highway.

Do you really think I care if you think I'm more than a little crazy?

Me, at the Route 66 Museum. Clinton, Oklahoma.

The U-Drop Inn. Shamrock, Texas.

7:50am. I slept well enough last night, retiring to bed at 11:00pm and not waking until 5:00am. I didn't crawl out of bed until 6:30am, as 5:00am is *far* too early to be up and about. Having said that, *had* I risen at that time, by now my writing (including the three postcards I've just forced myself to write) would all be *'done and dusted'*. Ah! But I'm in no hurry. It's only 8:00am, I have until 11:00am to check out and Lubbock is a mere 100 miles away. That's less than two hours driving time.

No. I decided (for reasons known only to my subconscious) to stay in bed, just contemplating life, the universe, my own mortality.........the usual shit.

Perhaps I crave sleep simply to escape the realities of a life that frightens me so much. For, in sleep, the world can be such a beautiful place. Sometimes (though sadly, not very often), in my dreams, I can fly. *Wow!* And, *Double Wow!* It's probably the greatest feeling I have ever experienced. Do *you* ever fly in your dreams?

This raises a very interesting question. Just what would a sleep analyst make of it?

Flights of fantasy, perhaps? Indicating that sometimes I'm in the habit of letting my imagination off the leash, that it may go whither it pleases (out on the town; living it up having a wild old time) only to return hung over and totally disillusioned with what it finds.

But, perhaps my flights are no more than my subconscious telling me what I already know. That is, that I would dearly love to get the hell out of here, *ASAP*.

I overate last night. Well. I'm on holiday. It happens.

Consequently, I have decided to give my system a well-earned break.

Breakfast. A small cup of apple juice, an equally small cup of orange juice and two cups of black coffee (with sugar). Well, I'm not *that* much of a martyr. No. I'm afraid that coffee would have to be of the highest quality to be drunk without sugar. And let's face it, they're hardly likely to supply such a product for free in a motel, now are they?

Apart from the bed, all the furniture in this room is metal. Sorry. There *is* one easy chair in the corner. It's totally amazing. For, were you not to touch it, you'd swear that it was a dark, expensive-looking wood.

The headboard is metal, as are the bedside tables, the coffee table, the writing desk and the large chest of drawers, on which sits the television and the microwave. Still. It's all very pleasing on the eye, and serves its purpose. Bravo.

The room itself is spacious and clean. All in all, value for money.

As I drive this interstate (Interstate 40), Route 66 is often glimpsed. Sometimes it's on the right, and sometimes it's on the left. On occasions, the old road will disappear into an underpass, only to re-emerge on the opposite side of the interstate. Then, several miles down the highway, the old road will use an overpass to traverse the *great highway.*

At times, it appears they are performing some strange dance, a mating ritual, like two huge snakes that have become intertwined. But I prefer to think of Route 66 as a boa constrictor, slowly trying to strangle the life out of the great beast that is the *'super slab'*, as Jerry McClanahan calls it.

Sadly, the old road concedes defeat and slinks off into the desert. But we know. Yes! *We* know (the friends of the old road), that it *will always* return.

Jerry McClanahan is (did I already tell you this?) the author of the EZ66 guide book, the updated version of which I purchased only yesterday. Oddly enough, it was only the same price as the one I purchased three or four years ago. I thought it would have been at least $2 more. So what do I say to that? *Bargain!* That's what I say.

Apart from not getting a picture of John Henry, as he tried to eat that mountain of food, (which, as you know, annoyed me no end) I was then stupid enough to pay my bill and leave, before finding out whether he had completed that incredible feat. It was only as I was walking to my car, that I realized my mistake. He can't have had much more than five minutes of his time left.

Did you know that if you fail to finish in the allotted one hour, the meal will cost you a mere $30?

Come On. It's got to be worth trying and failing for that price, hasn't it? I mean. 20 of our English pounds, for all that meat, shrimp cocktail, baked potato and a bread roll. I've said it before, and I'll say it again. *Bargain!*

But no. I love my food, it's true. But I much prefer to *'eat-to-live'*, rather than *'live-to-eat'*.

Yesterday's music.

Don't stop believing: Journey.

Sultans of Swing: Dire Straits. Now then. If I remember rightly, I was on a ship called the British Loyalty when I first heard this song. No. I can't recall the name of the bar off hand. However, I do know that it was somewhere in Durban, South Africa. Ah. Happy days.

Love Train: The Detroit Emeralds.

Come Together: The Beatles.

And Finally. A song I haven't heard since Adam was a lad and dinosaurs ruled the earth. But what a simply amazing, fantastic, out of this world song it is. Yes. Here's another one for you Youtube fans to look up. Oh! And while you're there, check the release date for me, would you? I'm pretty sure that it was 1970, but you know what my memory's like. Not what it used to be.

Indiana wants me: R. Dean Taylor.

7:40pm. Howard Johnson Motel. Corner of 48th Street and Avenue Q, Lubbock, Texas. Yes. I made it.

Actually, I've been here since 2:30pm. After checking in, I went straight next door to do my laundry, in what has to be, one of the largest laudromats in the entire universe. I'm terribly sorry, but I can't tell you how many washers and dryers they have, as there were just *too* many to count. Of course, in England, it would be called a launderette. But, as long as I get my washing done, what do I care what it's called?

Here we go. Listen to this. Small box of soap powder (all you need), clothes washed and dried: $2.94. Unbelievable.

I got the distance wrong, *again.*

It's not 100 miles from Amarillo to Lubbock, it's 130 miles. But hey! What's 30 miles between friends.

As I wasn't going be allowed to check in at this motel before 2:00pm, I decided to stop off in the town of Plainview on the way down.

Plainview is 47 miles north of Lubbock, and is where I spent two nights around this time last year. November 1st and 2nd, to be precise. Which means that it is a year to the day since I last stayed at this motel. You can't get more precise than that. Would you like to know something really, really, *really* interesting? Of course you would. Well, it cost $3.39 more per night last year, than I'm paying this year.

In Plainview, I made my way to the older part of town, which was where I encountered a lady, who, in last year's journal I referred to as *'Lucille'.* Well, I had to give her a name, didn't I? Those of you who've read last year's journal will be familiar with Lucille, and those of you who haven't............well............if you ask nicely, I might just let you borrow it. Alright?

Nothing had changed. The old Hilton was still the old Hilton, battered and bruised by years of neglect and vandalism, yet still standing proud.

I went looking for the coffee shop I had passed a year ago, and found it to be open on this occasion. *'Broadway Brew'.* A fine name for a coffee shop, wouldn't you say? *'An interesting looking place'*, thought I, so ventured inside.

Obviously, they had a variety of coffees, both hot and chilled.

Though my vanilla mocha was delicious to taste, it was neither hot nor chilled. 'Warm' would be the word I'd use to describe it.

With my warm coffee, I had a piece of carrot cake. And, at $6.32, I thought it a little overpriced.

I got the feeling that this place (like the Hilton) had been closed down for many a long year, though unlike the Hilton, because of its small size, was much easier to reopen.

Looking around I concluded that, in a former life (so to speak), it had been a diner of some sort and many of the fixtures were from that earlier time.

The stools at the counter were tarnished chrome, with red plastic seat covers. The counter was horseshoe shaped and, in its day, would have made an impressive focal point. Today, however, the paint (that in my opinion had not been professionally applied) only served to add insult to injury and make this probably once impressive diner look worse than if they'd just cleaned the place up. But that's the thing, you see. The owners (presumably on a tight budget, and not wanting to overspend on what might turn out to be a *loser*, business-wise) must have thought that a lick of paint would do the job. Who knows? Maybe if they make enough money out of it, they *may* just be able to restore it to its former glory.

I suspected that the booths (like the counter and stools) were original features. It's quite possible that the tables were too, though there were so many different styles of chair, *they* couldn't all be original, could they?

There were two sofas and one easy chair, which gave the place a more relaxed feel. Next to one of the sofas was an old chest, which, I guess, was used as a coffee table. The walls were light brown and cream. Curious.

Propeller fans kept the place cool, while several different types of lighting (one of which was a rather over-the-top chandelier, complete with cobweb) illuminated its interior.

Outside, and to the right of the building, was a patio. While on the window, a sign read: *'Thank you for not smoking on the patio'.* I wanted to shout out loud. *'It's outside, for pity's sake. Where else can the nicotine addict get his fix, if not outside?'* The patio furniture (not in use at this time) was chained together, lest anyone steal it.

More chairs and tables were strategically positioned at the front of the shop, as if as a means of saying to potential customers, *'Yes! We are open'*.

It's 9:15pm folks, and though I've a lot more to say, to be perfectly honest with you, I'd rather watch telly than keep writing this nonsense.

I don't have to worry about checking out, so I'll fill you in on the rest of the day's events in the morning. I trust you can wait until then? Oh, goodie!

Now where the hell did I put that remote?

The Old Hilton Hotel. Plainview, Texas.

The Big Texan. Amarillo, Texas.

WEDNESDAY NOVEMBER 4TH

8:25am. It certainly makes a change, not being up against the clock. It's not easy to concentrate when one is constantly looking to see how many hours or minutes are left to check-out time.

Still. Must look on the bright side. I could be doing this for a living, which would *really* stress me out.

Whilst wandering around old Plainview, I came across a fine old building (though it was empty, run down and had a *'to let'* sign in one of the windows) which had a date just above the top floor and a plaque on the front of the building. The date was 1912, and the plaque read: *'Entered in the national register of historic places, 1982'.*

Questions: Is the act of simply putting a building on a national register enough? Does it afford the building any special privileges? Will the simple act help maintain the building? Or, is it nothing more than a token gesture? You decide.

As I strolled around in the hot sunshine (Yes. This is Texas, where everything is bigger and better than anywhere else. Even the sun is hotter), I came across several second-hand shops, though, in these frugal times, it should come as no surprise to see such businesses thriving.

As if not wanting to be outdone by the second-hand shops, there was no shortage of finance companies offering loans.

Borrow money from the loan company, and then spend it in the second-hand shop. Yes. I can see the logic in that.

The year before last, while staying at the Super 8 Motel just a few miles north of here (still on the same street, Avenue Q, to be precise), I contemplated eating at River Smiths, which is just across the street from the motel. However, after walking in and looking around, I decided against it and settled instead for Denny's, which, as I recall, left a lot to be desired.

But, after skimming through the restaurant section of the phone book, I decided to give River Smiths a try. After all, do they not say, *'Never judge a book by its cover'?* I believe they do.

What happens is this: You order your food from the counter, you pay for it, they then give you an electronic device, which will buzz once your order is ready and then the food will be brought to your table. Simple.

Two catfish. Yes. That'll do for me. The meal (when it arrived) came with fries, coleslaw and a small bread roll, which, for reasons unknown, had been deep fried, like the fries and the catfish.

The sign specifically said, that you could have the catfish filleted if you so wished. And that is precisely what I asked for.

You see, I once had a very bad experience with whole catfish. It was in *'Catfish Kitchen'*, Dickson, Tennessee, though I don't recall what year that was. But the point is this. One *cannot* enjoy a meal, when one is constantly having to remove fish bones from one's mouth. Damned unpleasant.

So, having ordered my fillets of catfish, I found myself a table and waited patiently. After half an hour, I was getting a little irritated. Yes. It's true. I am a very patient man (when I need to be), but this was getting silly. I calmly walked over to the counter, enquired as to the whereabouts of my food and within 30 seconds, there it was. But the fish had not been filleted. No. All the chef (cook, or whatever) had done, was lay each fish on its side, take a knife and chop them into three pieces. Now, although I am not skilled in the art of filleting, I am intelligent enough to know that, *'To Fillet'* means to remove the flesh from the bone. *'Et voila.'*

The food, though not unpleasant to taste, was, nevertheless, overpriced ($15.05). Would I eat there again? Doubtful.

Am I being unkind? Maybe. However, I can only give this place 5/10, and I didn't leave a tip.

I have to admit, I'm a little nervous at the prospect of seeing Trish again. She wasn't very pleasant the last time we communicated. But, to this day, I have no idea why she got so shirty with me. I just hope we can clear the air and be friends again. Of course, if it's not to be…………well…………that's life.

Let's face it, I have far more important issues to deal with. If people like me, that's fine, and if they don't, well................'*fuck 'em'!*

I heard only one decent song yesterday, and that was the excellent *'Free Bird'*, by Lynyrd Skynyrd. *'Lynyrd Skynyrd'*. Can anyone tell me anything about the name?

Whether I see Trish or not is immaterial (no offence). But! What *does* concern me right now, is where the hell do I go in the morning?

I've thought about Las Vegas, San Francisco, or even Santa Monica, but I just don't know *what* to do. Think man, think. Where would you *really* like to go? Oh, I don't know. Pass. Next question, and make it an easy one this time.

If I were fortunate enough to win a trip to the moon, you can guarantee that some bastard would get there before me and construct a railway system that just happened to run past my accommodation. Ironically, this is one of the few motels I've stayed at where I have not been within earshot of a rail network. Having said that, I do quite like the sound of the trains as they pass by. But! Not when I'm trying to sleep.

11:00am. I won't go to the Buddy Holly Centre until this afternoon. 2:00pm sounds like a good time to me.

4:40pm. Well, that was a pretty successful afternoon, all things considered.

Although I'm not in the habit of eating lunch (as most lunch times I'm on the road), I saw an interesting sign. I'm so glad that I stopped in at *'Ranch House Restaurant'* this afternoon. It's what you might call a *'down to earth'* kind of a place that just serves delicious food, at a reasonable price. This *'treasure'* of a place is located on Buddy Holly Avenue, in Lubbock, Texas. I had the roast beef, with mashed potato, corn on the cob, gravy and a salad. This was followed by, spiced cake with ice cream and I washed the whole lot down with a glass of iced tea. Now you may not believe this, but, the bill for that marvellous meal, came to the ridiculously low price of $6.50. I know! I couldn't believe it myself. I've been in diners and restaurants that charged four times that amount, and the food wasn't *nearly* as good.

They say, *'You get what you pay for'*. Oh, no! Not necessarily.

8:40pm. I've not long got back from having a *very* late dinner. Yes. I know. It isn't good for me. But. What *is* good for me?

I've just tried a little experiment. I wanted to send an email to Trish, with a photo attached, but it didn't work. It works when I use conventional emailing, though I couldn't quite fathom out how to do it on the Internet. Damned out-going servers. Anyway. I don't understand. What the hell is a *'server'*? And more to the point, how do I change over to one that will let me send emails while I'm on my holidays?

Out-going servers? Bah! Humbug! To me, it's just another one of those *'Great mysteries of the universe'*. I hate this world.

Did I ever tell you about the time I was in Cairo? No? Could've sworn I did. Are you sure it wasn't you? I guess it must have been someone else. Memory's going.

9:00pm. I'm feeling a little strange. Neutralized. Yeah. That's it. I'm feeling sad. No! Not sad. Indifferent. Oh, I don't fucking know. *'HELP!'*

Me and my good friend Trish. The Buddy Holly Centre, Lubbock, Texas.

7:55am. Hey! I've just realized. It's Guy Fawkes night. Or, as we always called it when I was a kid, *'Bonfire Night'*. But where does the word *'Bonfire'* come from? Now, we all know that 'Bon' is French for good. But. *'Goodfire Night'?* Possibly. But what's good about it? And when (exactly) did the tradition of Bonfire Night start?

Now, although you may not have learned anything from this, I certainly made you think, did I not?

I'm feeling a little better this morning, though still at a loss as to where I should go.

Ah! Now then. If I head back to Holbrook, Arizona, I can revisit the Painted Desert and Petrified Forest.

Unfortunately, on my previous visit I arrived late in the afternoon, consequently I had very little time in which to wander off and explore the many trails in that area.

I exchanged several text messages with Trudy last night. The upshot is that we *may* be taking a trip to Las Vegas together, someday. Next year? Well, if she can arrange to be on vacation on my next visit to Dickson, then yes. Nothing wrong with two friends taking a road trip together, is there? No. Of course there isn't. Other people do it all the time, I'm sure.

I didn't eat until very late last night. 7:45pm, to be precise.

Denny's. I haven't had much success with Denny's, of late. Which is why I was pleasantly surprised with the dish I ordered. *'Prime Rib Sizzling Skillet'*.

The beef came with hash browns, topped with cheese, sautéed onions and peppers, three tortilla wraps, salsa and sour cream. And for those of you *not in the know*, one simply puts the beef, salsa and sour cream into the wrap, rolls it up, pops it into a jiffy bag and sends it off to someone more needy. No! Stop! That's *my* dinner.

And, at $11.89, plus a $2 tip, well worth the money. Well done Denny's. You've gone up in my estimation.

As I left Denny's, and headed for my car, I saw a black guy sitting on the low wall outside the diner. Though he called to me, at first, I just ignored him. But then, something made me stop. I turned and faced him. *"Can you spare a few dollars sir?"* he asked. So, I pulled out the small, plastic bag I always carry, containing my loose change. On seeing how little was in the bag, I returned it to my pocket and instead, pulled out a wad of notes. *'Should I give him two, or three? No. I'll give him five.'* I thought to myself.

I handed him the $5 bill and, although he thanked me, he then asked me for a further $3. I have to say that I was more than a little annoyed at this point, and told him not to be so greedy. Though he wasn't threatening, it did cross my mind, that at any moment, he *could* produce a knife and threaten me with it. I turned and carried on my way towards my car, with him trailing closely behind, all the while begging for more money. As I got into my car and locked the door, he stood there, gesturing for me to wind the window down, but I ignored him.

But who was this sad, pathetic looking man? And why is it, that he (and so many others) has to live like this? *Surely*, there's enough to go round.

As I pulled out of the parking lot, I turned to see him throwing up (vomiting, spewing, puking up). Whatever way you put it, the guy was sick. But not sick in any conventional way. No. This guy was a drug addict. Wasn't he? Am I just making an assumption? Jumping to a conclusion? I'll never know.

As I drove back to the motel, I was angry. After all, had I not tried to do him a kindness? How many others had just walked on by, before I came along? Yet, my generosity was not enough.

But now. Yes. Right now. Here, in the cold light of dawn, in my comfortable motel room, it all looks so very different. $5, or $5,000. It wouldn't have changed his plight. I know it's a bit of a cliché, but money just isn't the answer. What these people need is help. There's so much more I'd like to say on this subject, but I just can't find the right words.

And now for something completely different. Okay! So I'm a plagiarist. Who isn't? Here's one for you trivia buffs: What was Buddy Holly's real name? Oh! I'm so sorry. Were you expecting me to give you the answer? It was merely a question. I *was* hoping that *you* could tell me. Oh, come on. When are you going to realize that I have a strange (some would say, *'playful'*) sense of humour.

CHARLES HARDIN (BUDDY) HOLLEY
BORN: SEPTEMBER 7TH 1936.

The observant among you will notice that his actual surname has an E in it.

Trish. Yes, that's my one-time penfriend, then ex-penfriend, and now, once again penfriend. Oh, what a strange life I lead.

After a silence of approximately eight months, we are now on speaking terms again. No. Not just on speaking terms, as that seems to suggest that we are merely being civil to one another. Oh no. It's far more than that. Actually, we *are* good friends once again. Now isn't that nice?

We spent two very pleasant hours, practically talking non stop. Okay. She was talking. I was listening. *'I'm Joking!'* I did manage to get a *few* words in. ha ha.

7:25pm. Grants, New Mexico.

I haven't been in Grants since the old days. Yep. If memory serves, I've stayed in this town on at least two other occasions (possibly three), but that was early on in my road tripping days (2001 and 2002). EE-BY-GUM. *'That were back when cars were cars, and men were made of steel and ships were made of wood and'*......I don't half talk some rubbish at times.

Steadily moving on.

All in all, it's been a pretty good day.

But the highlight, oh yes, the highlight has to be Dinner. I'm staying at a Travelodge Motel (the closest motel to the interstate), which has a Denny's within spitting distance. But, it was not to that establishment that I went to silence the rumbling in my tummy. Oh, no. For some strange reason, I decided to browse the

Travelodge manual. (Such a manual can be found in all motels and gives information such as, local churches, garages, *attorneys* and restaurants.) It was during my *browse*, that my eyes were drawn to '*La Ventana Restaurant*'. Now, had I not been given directions to this place, I would never have found it.

La Ventana, is about a mile and a half from the motel. The lady at reception told me to look out for Pizza Hut, and just before it, I was to turn right, down Geis. (No! It doesn't say street or road, just Geis.) Geis is just one short block, at the bottom of which (and over to the right) can be found a rather plain looking, windowless and totally uninviting building. The establishment was not illuminated in any way, and the car park, though half full, was only dimly lit (and you know what I think about dimly lit car parks).

However, anxious to calm my rumbling tummy, I ventured inside. What a transformation! Though its interior was as dimly lit as its exterior, on entering, I found the place to be warm and inviting.

To me, it was the height of sophistication, a place where one would expect to find only the '*well heeled and keeled*', though this was not the case.

The place was a total contradiction.

Here was this magnificent restaurant with crisp white tablecloths, linen napkins, an extensive wine list and a menu of the highest order (in my opinion) and yet at the bar sat two guys in very casual clothing, drinking beer from the bottle, while at one of the tables sat eight adults and two small children, one of whom cried rather a lot. One of the guys at this particular table wore a baseball cap, while the other wore a cowboy hat. It was so absurd. And yet, that is precisely the way it should be.

When I looked at the menu, I thought it a little pricey, though no more so than Red Lobster, and you know what I thought of that.

I started with a cup of (Cup = small. Bowl = big. Remember?) chilli con queso. (Imagine chilli without the meat, but with lots of cheese.) I was also served a large basket of tortilla chips, with a spicy tomato sauce.

Next came the main course. I decided to push the boat out on this one. Oh, yes. *"You only live once"*, as I told the waitress. So I went for the Prime Rib, 21 day hung, Angus Steak. Rare. Well, I thought I'd died and gone to heaven. A tastier piece of beef you could not find. Tasty as tasty could be. Tender as tender could be and served with a tangy horseradish sauce, broccoli and cauliflower. The meal included two bread rolls and as much Pepsi as I could drink. And the price? A mere $26.78, which is less than 17 English pounds. I quite happily left $32. As for marks out of ten, it has to be 9½.

And let me tell you this. I *do* feel a little guilty about not awarding it a 10. But what can I do? I've nothing to compare it to. Yet, if by the end of this road trip, I find no better food than that of *La Ventana,* then I shall certainly upgrade it to a 10. Now I can't say fairer than that, can I?

The trip from Lubbock to Grants was a total of 478 miles. There really isn't that much to say about it. I did stop for gas after about 150 miles, put $20 worth in and I had just about enough to get me here.

The motel is $66.93 per night. That's more than I would want to be paying, but the room's alright.

To round the evening off (and send you to sleep with that warm, cosy feel), here are today's sounds from the airwaves:

You send me: Sam Cook.

Don't bring me down: E.L.O.

I only wanna be with you: (No. It's not the Dusty Springfield one, though I really do love that song. Come to think of it, Dusty did sing some wonderful songs.) Hootie and the Blowfish.

Groovy kind of love: (I love it. It's a very special song for me.) Phil Collins.

Every breath you take: The Police.

Borderline: (the only other decent song she's sung) Mad Donna.

Don't wanna miss a thing: (another song that I really love) Aerosmith.

I should have known better: (if I had to pick a favourite Beatles song, this would be it. Closely followed by, *I wanna hold your hand*.) The Beatles. I'm filling up already.

FRIDAY NOVEMBER 6ᵀᴴ

8:30am. If there is one reason I'll be glad to get home, it is so that I shall once again be able to send *normal* emails. Going via the Internet, which gives one a mere 15 minute window in which to compose and send one's emails is (if you'll pardon my French) a real pain in the arse.

That has to be the best night's sleep I've had since I started this *'marathon of motel stays'*, also known as a *'road trip'*.

Though awake by 6:00am, I lay there for over an hour, wondering whether Las Vegas was a good idea. If you remember, the last time I was there I *did* start to slip. Or, as I described it back then (2007), *'I was beginning to stagnate'*. Being in the one place for any length of time just isn't good for me, or so it would seem. Do I *need* a companion on my road trips? Good question.

I texted Trudy the other day, enquiring about her health. You see, she hadn't been well. *'Sick as a dog'*, as she put it.

I told her that I was *probably* heading for Las Vegas, and she informed me that it was a place she had always wanted to visit. I replied, saying that maybe we could go together sometime, to which she replied, *'Maybe we can do that'*. The final text came from me, saying, *'Yeah. Maybe we can'*. So it looks like me and Trudy could well be doing a road trip together. Knowing my luck, we'd probably end up like some fucking modern-day *'Bonnie and Clyde'*, on the run from the police and having to sleep in the car or an old barn. Of course, then I'd have to ditch the rental car and steal one. *'I can't steal a car. I wouldn't know how to.'* Admittedly, it would be quite easy to hide. I mean, America *is* a big place. But how would we live? Where would we get money from? No. That's no kind of a life, is it? Stop! Stop! Stop! What am I talking about? My imagination is running riot. Oh, Gawd. I feel another Victor Meldrew moment coming on.

Anyway. Watch this space. This time next year, I may well be writing about how Trudy spends too long in the shower, or *insists* on us sleeping in a *'smoking room'*. Yes. Trudy smokes. Hey! Wait a

145

minute. Wait-just-one-cotton-picking-minute. Who said we'd be sharing a room? Again. Knowing my luck, every motel we tried, they'd probably say the same thing, *'I'm terribly sorry, but apart from one smoking room, which I'm afraid has a dodgy shower, we are fully booked.'* AAAAAAARGH!

'There you go again with the negative waves, Moriarty.' Another line by Donald Sutherland's character *'Oddball'*, from that excellent movie *'Kelly's Heroes'*.

Hey! I just got a refund.

Now, as a rule, I'm not one for reading small print. But, for reasons known only to God (let's face it, I have absolutely no idea why I do what I do), I decided to read the small print on my motel receipt. It informed me of the fact that, a charge of $1.50 had already been added to my bill, for use of the safe in my room, and may be removed upon request at check-out. Now then. You tell me. How many people actually read that small print and then claim back their $1.50? It gets better. I actually received $1.69. That's the $1.50, plus 19 cents tax. You may mock. But it's the principle, and it all adds up.

In Rapid City, they charged $1.12 per night for use of the in-room safe, though it was not refunded on check-out.

I wouldn't mind paying for the use of an in-room safe, but the idiot who was in here before me locked it and then checked out. No! I can't go and ask for a spare key, it's a digital lock. Still. If you were to throw a cloth over it and put a vase of flowers on it, it would make an ideal occasional table, which, if you ever managed to unlock it, could *occasionally* be used as a safe. *Doh!*

I left my room at about 7:45am and headed for the lobby to see what breakfast delights were on offer. As per usual, I started with the Raisin Bran, followed by two pieces of toast with peanut butter, a chocolate muffin and two cups of coffee. The coffee wasn't up to much, but let's face it, where would I be without it?

Driving to and from the restaurant last night, I passed a profusion of independently run motels. But in a town the size of Grants, which obviously has a lot to offer the tourist, I would imagine that there would be no shortage of guests to fill the rooms in these establishments.

Though *I* prefer to stay at one of the major chains, it is comforting for someone like me (a friend of the old road) to see so many of these long established motels, still thriving. Maybe it's time I started patronizing some of these smaller motels. Just the odd one, here and there.

Oh! I'm sorry. Did I fail to mention the fact that Grants, New Mexico is on Route 66? Can you manage to read this yourself, or would you like me to do that for you as well? I don't know. Some people.

The Arizona state line is about 80 miles west of here, while a further 80 miles on is the town of Holbrook, which is where I based myself only the year before last when I visited the Painted Desert and Petrified Forest.

Now, should I go back to Holbrook before visiting Las Vegas, or stop off there on the way back to Tennessee?

Question: Why in the hell am I going to Vegas anyway? What could possibly be there for me?

I'm supposed to be enjoying myself, but I'm not. *Why?* What the fuck is wrong with me?

10:05am. Check-out's at 11:00am. Have I time to send a couple of emails?

I know. I won't do too much driving today. I'll check into a motel early (somewhere) and then send my emails. There. You *can* make decisions when you really, really need to.

4:25pm. Williams, Arizona.

Two years ago, I stayed at a Motel 6 in this town, and it cost me $61.45. *'Wow! What an incredible memory you have.'* No. Not really. I've just checked my records. On this occasion, I plumped for a Days Inn (my third of the trip, to be precise) and at $66.21 per night, I'd say it was pretty good value.

As you know, I've stayed at a number of motels where they have been good enough to provide an in-room safe. But! This particular motel provides an in-room......wait for it, wait for it……wall safe. No! No! No! It's not hidden behind a portrait of the *'Mona Lisa'.* Can you not be serious for one minute?

I've got two large beds in my room. So, if anyone's in need of a bed for the night, you know where to come. Now, which one shall I sleep in? Eeny, meeny, miny, mo. Oh, sod it. I'll have the one nearest to the telly.

At the motel in Grants, the pool was open 24 hours a day. *'Is that odd?'* Well, yes it is, actually. All the motels I've stayed at in the past have insisted that no one be allowed to swim after 10:00pm.

Next to the pool was a hot tub, though some idiots must have thought it was a wishing well, hence the pennies in it. If brains were dynamite, I swear, they wouldn't have enough to blow their flaming noses with.

I *could* drive into the village for dinner, but the streets are narrow and there are a lot of one-way systems, so I'll settle for good old Denny's, which just happens to be within walking distance. Now, aren't I lucky?

I referred to Williams as a village rather than as a town, as it is so small and compact. Unlike most of the towns I've stayed in, it's perfect for walking around and sightseeing. Not that I'll be wandering around or doing any sightseeing, as I'll be moving on in the morning.

Did you know you can catch a train from here all the way up to the Grand Canyon Village? Well, you do now. It's only a distance of about 60 miles.

As I walked out of my motel room at 7:45am (in search of 'eats'), though the sun was out, there was a chill in the air. But this was New Mexico, and three hours later (when I was ready to check out), the sun was high and I could tell that it was going to be another fine day.

I'll tell you something. It's a bloody good job that Colorado wasn't on my itinerary. Those poor buggers up there got two foot of snow, and it's not even winter yet.

As I drove the 350miles or so, from Grants to Williams, the old road kept appearing, as if beckoning me to join her, but I resisted the temptation. But why? What the hell's in Las Vegas that I'm in such a rush to get there? Is there something (or someone) waiting for me?

Yes. The pull of the old road is strong, but right now, Las Vegas is stronger.

I've just had a thought. If I were to take a friend on a road trip with me, I could be their tour guide and impress them with my knowledge of all the places we'd visit. So what do you think of that? Yeah. You're probably right. *'Someone else in the car with me?'* No. It would never work.

I came close to running out of gas. I was nothing more than 20 miles east of Flagstaff, and I probably would have made it all the way there, but with this new gas, that doesn't give the same mileage as the regular unleaded, I didn't want to take a chance, so I pulled off the road in Winona, just as the 'low fuel' warning appeared. Bad move. The gas was $2.99. Expensive. So, I just put $4 worth in and another $20 worth when I reached Flagstaff. The gas in Flagstaff was $2.79. Though still a little pricey, it could have been worse, I could have filled the tank in Winona.

I suppose you're wondering why I didn't stop at Holbrook, or the Painted Desert. What do you mean, *'No we're not'?* Would it kill you to show just a *little* interest?

5:40pm. That's it. You've upset me now. I'm off to Denny's. *You* can get your own tea. Bye!

7:00pm. Denny's. My one time favourite place to eat, though I fear it will never again reach that pinnacle.

The meal started off well enough, but went right downhill after that.

The surroundings were pleasant enough, as were the staff. However, the quality of the food and the prices, just weren't in sync. So sad.

I started off with the *'sampler'*. Strips of chicken in batter (deep fried), onion rings in batter (deep fried) and cheese sticks in batter (deep fried). These came with four dips. Honey mustard, barbecue, spicy tomato, and ranch. How can I describe the ranch dip? Well, I guess it's like a cheese flavoured dip. That's all I can say. Oh! Apart from, *'it really is quite tasty'*.

I then opted for the fish and chips, with tartare sauce and coleslaw.

The waitress informed me that, *"The fish is all-you-can-eat."* I sat there staring at her, with a totally bemused look on my face, all the while thinking, *'No it isn't. I can eat whatever I like, thank you very much'*. Totally amazing. The woman must have been able to read my mind, or at least, decipher my puzzled look, for she went on to say, *"No, no. What I mean is, you can eat as much as you like for the one set price."*

Only in America. The meal was $22.27, plus a $3 tip. Excessive.

The starter was.........not bad.........I guess. But as for that fish. Well, I have absolutely no idea what kind of fish it was, but I wouldn't have wanted any more, even if I had still been hungry, which I wasn't. All that deep fried, battered food, just made my stomach swell. No. I should have gone for the T-bone. But, I had steak last night, so I wanted something different. *'Something different? You got that alright.'*

I think it's time we had some music, don't you? Yes. That's just what the doctor ordered. You know? I'm baffled as to why I haven't been able to pick up any of those *oldies* stations on this trip. I've never had a problem in the past. So, where are they? Oh, sure, I hear the occasional decent record, but I'm used to listening to radio stations that specialize in things like, *'The Sounds of the Sixties'*. All those sounds that go *way* back. If you've been paying attention (and I hope for your sake you have, because there's a 'question and answer' session at the end of this class), you'll know what I mean.

Now, although I can't claim to be a big fan of this group, they have, nevertheless, written (and sung) some really great songs.

How deep is your love: The Bee Gees.

Africa: Toto.

Moody Blue: (The King) Elvis Presley.

You belong to me: I've heard this song several times since I arrived, and I have to admit, it gets better every time I hear it. Taylor Swift.

All over now: The Rolling Stones.

Sweet home Alabama: Lynyrd Skynyrd. (Hannah likes this one. Me? I prefer *Free Bird*.)

Maggie May: (again) Rod Stewart.

Won't back down: Tom Petty and the Heartbreakers.

Now that *is* amazing. No. Seriously. It's only 8:15pm and I'm finished. Most nights, I'm writing until nine, or even ten and even then I'm not finished. I guess there's a lot to be said for checking into a motel early.

I've probably forgotten something of great importance. But, if it should come to me whilst watching telly, you can be sure that I'll rush straight over to the computer, switch it on and inform you of it post-haste.

Yeah. Right. You can wait until the morning......and like it. What do you think you're on, Daddy's yacht?

8:10 am. Damn, damn and thrice damn.

Wouldn't you just know it? I've gone and left my shaving oil back in Grants. It's too far to go back, so I guess I'll just have to buy some when I get to Vegas. Yes! I said Vegas. My two day stay in Vegas is all sorted.

I'm just so proud of myself. It was a bit like the time, oh, you know, when you realize that you can actually ride a bicycle without falling off, or stay afloat in the swimming pool. Yes. It was one of those *Eureka* moments. *'I. Me. Moi.'* Yes! I *actually* made a booking online. Can you imagine my elation on receiving the confirmation email? I was *so* elated in fact, that had there been anyone in the room with me at the time, I would surely have kissed them (providing it was a female, of course).

I got onto the Howard Johnson website last night, and filled in the reservation form for a four night stay, but then I bottled it. What if, when I got there, I didn't like the place? Would I be allowed to check out after just one night, without being charged for all four?

But as I lay in bed this morning, contemplating life, the universe and my role on this planet, I suddenly had a brainwave.

I leaped out of bed (okay, okay, I crawled out of bed. Is that better? Strewth. Some people are never satisfied), rushed over to my computer, fired up the beast and set to work on booking my *two* day stay in Las Vegas. (A small point, I know. But you may have noticed that I sometimes refer to Las Vegas simply as 'Vegas'. But then, I'm a seasoned traveller and you're not, so it's perfectly acceptable for me to do so.)

On accessing the Howard Johnson web site last evening, I was a little shocked at the price they were charging, $64, plus tax. That would have been in excess of $70 per night and, over four nights on my budget, just a little too pricey. However, when I booked and then received my confirmation email, I discovered, to my delight, that it was only for the Saturday that they would be charging $64. Oh, yes. Wait for it. On Sunday, the price drops down to a mere $44, plus tax. Now what do you think of that? As soon as I arrive (providing the accommodation is suitable, of course), I shall enquire as to the possibility of perhaps staying on for a extra few days. Yes?

9:00am. It doesn't matter what time I leave, for I know that there will definitely be a room at the inn for me tonight.

Should my plans change, and I decide not to go to Vegas, I have until 4:00pm to cancel my reservation. However, should I fail to cancel by 4:00pm, why then, I would be charged for one night (Saturday) and the charge would appear on my next credit card statement. Seems fair enough to me.

So, what could make me change my plans? At this point, my brow furrows, my eyes narrow, while my mind (like an old computer with a *very* slow search engine) ponders the imponderables.

Three hours later. *'That's it! I could......walk out of here...... yes......meet the woman of my dreams.........okay.........run off to Vegas with her, get married and live happily ever after.' Doh!* I'd still be in Vegas, wouldn't I?

Anyway. What are the chances? About as much as me striking it big in Vegas.

Back to the drawing board. Damn! Where did I put the drawing board?

'Cairo seems like such a long time ago, now.' *'Well of course it does, you idiot. It was 33 years ago.'*

I seem to recall someone once saying (though I know not who) that you should never mix numbers and letters. But why? What difference does it make? Does it confuse the reader? Do I give a shit?

33. Thirty three. What's the fucking difference? To me, it's the same.

Now then. For those of you who are expecting (at some point) to come across *pretty pictures* in this journal, then I suggest you stop reading now. Having said that, I *may* insert a few pictures at the end, but only to fill out the journal, as it were. Thus making it appear larger than it actually is. No! It's not cheating. It's not me that wants pictures in the damn thing, it's you.

Whilst it may be true that, *'every picture tells a story',* and whilst it may also be true that, *'a picture paints a thousand words',* answer me this question: Who among you would prefer to look at my holiday snaps, rather than read my *meagre offering* to the world of literature? Come on. Be honest. I won't bite.

Second question: Who among you had to think for more than two seconds before answering that question? Shame on you.

9:50am. Let's go to Vegas, and see what we can find.

4:10pm. The Howard Johnson Inn, Las Vegas.

I've stayed in worse. But then, I've been fortunate enough to stay in *far* better. This establishment (hotel, motel, inn, or whatever it's classed as) is across the road from Econo Lodge, a motel I have stayed at on three occasions, in the dim and distant past. (I wonder if they've cleaned that carpet yet?) It is, however, just slightly closer to where all the action is. By that, I mean all the major hotels and casinos.

My room (though small) is adequate, with a functional safe and *even* a sliding door that leads out onto a patio (my patio), from where I can walk straight across a small patch of grass and have direct access to the swimming pool. So, if it's warm enough, I shall be taking a dip before breakfast. I've always wanted to do that.

It would appear that they don't do a free breakfast, though they do have a restaurant *and* a bar. Yeah. Like it really was worth mentioning the bar.

The only way you'll get *me* in that bar is if I'm dead and someone with a really sick sense of humour invites me to my own wake.

I would dearly love to write, but my mind's gone blank. I don't even want to follow that last sentence with a humorous remark.

I'm hungry, but it's only 5:00pm. Too early to eat. Ah! Now then. Reception. Perhaps they could tell me a little about the restaurant.

Though (as you *probably* already know) Vegas has a profusion of hotels, with no shortage of eateries within them, I do feel slightly uncomfortable in those places. I can't explain why exactly, I just do.

I need somewhere close, but not too over-the-top. Can you recommend anywhere?

Denny's is just down the road, but after last night, I don't know if I should risk another Denny's so soon.

I know! I'll have a shower and a shave, put on a clean shirt and go for a wander. How does that sound? Good. Let's see what's on offer.

Hey! You should see the cabinet that's housing my telly. Got to be worth a bob or two. In fact, it's probably worth more than all the other furniture in this room put together.

7:50pm. Las Vegas! You've just restored my faith in Denny's. I've just had a beautiful meal. Beautiful? Delicious? Who cares?

Denny's of Las Vegas gets an 8½ out of 10.

The place has changed so much since my last visit. Back then (2007), I'd just come from Kingman, Arizona, where I was unfortunate enough to encounter one of the biggest cowboys in the history of American dentistry, but we'll say no more about that as this is a family show. Okay. So I swear from time to time. Doesn't everybody?

Leaving the motel, I headed south (uptown, as they say in Vegas) and passed a couple of wedding chapels, Boston's Pizza, a tattoo parlour (now, would someone kindly explain to me, just *how* in the world the words, *tattoo* and *parlour* have become connected? It's like, day and night, dark and light, chalk and cheese), the Oasis motel, with its *adult movies* and *fantasy suites* (I'm not at all sure what they mean by *fantasy suites*, but it might be worth checking out) and a place called 'O G', that advertises topless cabaret. As I passed it, I said to myself, '*When was the last time you had an alcohol-free Lager?*' And. '*Couldn't you just do with one now?*' I must admit, I *was* tempted. But there are plenty of ways to satisfy one's needs in Vegas, and paying a small fortune for a non alcoholic beverage, just to see some *young bird* (who, by the way, is *totally* off the menu. 'Look, but don't touch') *strutting her stuff*, is not, in my opinion, the most productive way of spending one's Saturday night. *'Oh yeah! So what did you have in mind?'* *'Okay. I've no idea where I'm going. But It's still not to O G.'*

I crossed the street, expecting to see Denny's car park absolutely packed, as it usually was (except for early in the morning). But no. Though there were several cars outside, there was only one patron inside, and as far as I could see, he was just sat there tapping away on his laptop. I *assumed* he'd already eaten. No. This was not a good sign. Did the cars belong to the staff? I guessed so.

As I walked in, I was greeted by a sign that read, *'Please wait to be seated'*. Why? Were they expecting three coachloads from Manchester? *'I'm terribly sorry, sir, but we couldn't possibly accommodate you. As you can see, this one customer is running us all ragged.'* Where do I get this rubbish from? Sometimes. Just sometimes. My imagination works overtime.

But I'm English, you see. And, for the most part, we like to play by the rules. So, like a lemon, I stood there, waiting to be seated.

"Just the one, sir?" the guy says to me. *"Er, no."* says I. *"I'm with the three coachloads from Manchester."* No. I couldn't be that cruel.

He showed me to my table and, before sitting down I bored him with tales of my travels. He listened patiently, though I could tell that he didn't really care and was just being polite. Why do I do it? Why must I insist on telling everyone I meet about my escapades, as though I were the only person in the world who ever does any travelling? I did the same thing as I was leaving. I went over to the cashier to settle my bill, and I started again. Just like the waiter, she too was polite, but she'd probably heard it all a thousand times before. *'Shut up, mister tourist. I really don't care.'* Well, I imagine that's what she was thinking. And who can blame her?

Now usually, the waiter (or waitress) will ask you what you want to drink, which is why I was so surprised to see the waiter come over, carrying a pot of coffee. *"The coffee's just been made. Would you like some?"* he asked. I thanked him and said yes. Well, a change is as good as a rest, as they say. Anyway, this was decent coffee, not the free stuff they give you in the motels.

I had to be careful not to order anything too greasy, or fatty.

It didn't take me long to spot the healthy option. Chicken noodle soup, with crackers, followed by prime rib steak salad, garlic bread and Italian dressing. Oh, yes. That hit the spot alright. I can honestly say that after that meal, I was a very happy bunny indeed.

Along with three cups of coffee, I was overjoyed to see that the bill was a paltry $15.21. I left the waiter a $3 tip, paid the bill and headed home.

Denny's, with the Stratosphere in the background.

6:40am. I've been awake since just before 6:00am, when I was roused from my slumber by a strange, light tapping sound on the wall. The light tapping slowly built to a much louder banging noise, which culminated in several groans. Yep. They were at it. The couple in room 112 were busy checking out the headboard, making sure that it was fully functional and enjoying an early morning *romp*.

Meanwhile, directly above me, the guy (girl?) moved around the room with the touch of a baby elephant No. Better make that, *full grown elephant*. With every thud, thud, thud, my ceiling creaked, creaked, creaked. It really was quite unnerving. Why, at any moment, the occupant of what I assumed was room 210 (my room is 110), could have dropped in for a chat. Literally.

Should I stay for two more nights?

In theory, it should be quieter after tonight, as Vegas is well known (along with many other cities) as a haven for those who just want a weekend away.

As the saying goes: *'What happens in Vegas, stays in Vegas'*.

When I checked in, I was given a card for the Florida Café Cuban Bar & Grill, which doubles as the motel restaurant. This entitles me to breakfast, for $5. I may as well go to Denny's.

It's light out now, but I'd like to sleep. Not much chance of that though. Already, I hear the sounds of movement, people stirring from their slumber, while others chatter like schoolgirls as they head down the corridor to the lobby to check-out, or to the restaurant to check out the menu.

Shower? Maybe. Don't need a shave. Had one last night.

Should I put the "do not disturb" sign on the door?

The door. It doesn't fit properly. There is *at least* a two inch gap at the bottom of my door, which doesn't improve the soundproofing in this room.

I wonder if it's worth checking out the prices of one of the major hotels. Is that a question? I don't know. But, *'Is that a question?'* is a question. Oh, how very droll.

'Caesar's Palace'. Ah! Now you're talking. I've always fancied staying there.

Of course, if I *were* to stay at Caesar's, I wouldn't get any reward points. Right now, I couldn't give a flying fuck. I've stayed in too many dives. *Surely!* I'm worth more than this.

I know. I'll just have a wash, brush my teeth and then see what culinary delights are on the breakfast menu. I can always shower after breakfast, can't I?

Hey! Something's just occurred to me. What if this voucher (ticket) entitles me to a breakfast to the value of no more than $5. Aha! Now that would make sense. After all, they weren't specific when they handed it to me. When I say *they*, what I mean is, that while one of the ladies at reception was dealing with my reservation, the other was handing me the voucher. So what do you think? Ah! Now then! It *must* mean that I am entitled to $5 worth of breakfast. You see, if I wanted to eat more than $5 worth, *then* and only *then* would I have to pay the over-and-above. Isn't it simply amazing how the human brain works? I've often thought so.

7:40am. It would appear that I have made a mistake. Two mistakes, to be precise. Unfortunately, I am not entitled to $5 worth of breakfast. Apparently, my voucher simply means, that as a resident of this motel, I can pick one of the breakfasts from the $5 section of the menu......and then pay $5 for it. Oh, how wonderful. And the second mistake? My watch was an hour fast. Yes. I crossed another time zone and didn't realize it. I *do* remember seeing a clock as I crossed the Hoover Dam, and I thought then that *it* must be wrong, an hour slow.

Every motel I've stayed at thus far, has had a radio alarm clock in the room, except this one.

I've just checked out the prices at Caesar's Palace, and I certainly won't be staying there. They want $140 before tax, *and* they charge for Internet access, just like the Days Inn Hotel in Newark, if you remember. I'd stay at Caesar's if I had more money. I guess I'd better get down to the casino and win a few bob on the slots.

It looks like I've got two choices. Either I book in here for another two nights, or I move on in the morning.

Even in Vegas. Even in bloody Vegas. What's that sound I can hear? Oh, yes. That would be the sound of a fucking train. *AAAAAAAAAAAAAAAAAARGH!* Yes! I know! I *did* say that I liked the sound of trains. But! There is a bloody limit.

8:01am. Breakfast.

Why did I put 8:01am? Why not 8:00am? Simple. Because when I looked at the clock, it was showing 8:01am. Is that alright with you?

Yesterday, I said that the only way you'd get me in that bar, would be if I were dead.

So. There I am, sitting in the Cuban restaurant section of the hotel bar, listening to a Spanish radio station, waiting patiently for my $5 breakfast that, wait for it, wait for it, costs *more* than $5.

The waitress brought me a cup of coffee, that I foolishly added artificial sweetener to. What a foul taste. I drank my coffee as fast as I could and hoped that it wouldn't take the waitress too long before realizing my cup needed refilling. I desperately needed to rid myself of that vile taste.

There was a choice of four breakfasts, none of which (as I would find out later) included coffee, tax, or a tip.

I opted for the French toast, with eggs (over easy) and ham. The French toast came with butter and as much maple syrup as I could manage.

The meal (when it arrived) was on a plate that was neither oval nor oblong, but somewhere in-between.

The plate rattled irritatingly atop the glass-covered table as I ate. Though I tried to silence the offending piece of crockery, it was to no avail. Fortunately, however, the radio was loud enough to muffle the noise, making me feel slightly less embarrassed.

9:50am. I'm so sorry to have to interrupt this fascinating tale about breakfast in a Cuban restaurant (within a hotel bar), but it would appear that the couple in the next room have just woken up and, are once again, ensuring that the headboard is still functioning as it should.

I finished my meal, which, though not the finest breakfast I had ever eaten, was nonetheless, of a reasonable standard.

The bill. Breakfast: $5. Coffee: $1.80. Tax: 55 cents. Total, including tip: $9. I shall go to Denny's tomorrow. It may well cost more, but when $5 becomes $7.35 (without the tip), I get a bit miffed.

I made one stop on the way here yesterday. I was about 8 miles east of Kingman, Arizona, and although I still had half a tank of gas, I put $10 worth in, thus ensuring that I wouldn't need to fill the tank before leaving Vegas.

Music. I haven't told you about yesterday's music. So here goes.

Summer in the city: Was that the Spencer Davis Group? Big Al would know. Big Al knows more about music than anyone I've ever met (popular music, that is). But who's Big Al? Ah! That would be Alan Howard. A gentleman, a scholar and a bloody good bloke. I'm proud to call him a friend.

Why can't this be love: White Snake. (I think)

And whilst I was in Denny's, only last night,

Life on Mars: David Bowie.

Cruel to be kind: Nick Lowe. I've said it before and I'll say it again, if you're not familiar with this song (or even if you are), then get onto YouTube, and listen to any one of several versions by this artist. Having said that, I don't think he wrote it.

10:30am. I think I'll have a lie down for a while, and then head uptown.

7:20pm. I've gone and done it.

I've checked in for another two nights. Mistake? Maybe. But sometimes, I get tired of being on the road. Oh, sure. I'm a complete fucking contradiction. *Most of the time*, I just love being on the road.

This motel, hotel, inn, or whatever it is, has its own wedding chapel. It's called the *'Shalimar Wedding Chapel'*, and there is obviously a wedding going on right now, as I have just heard them playing the wedding march.

If I ever decide to get married.........What am I saying? Calm down! I only said *'IF'*. But if I did, Las Vegas would be as good a place as any to do it, right?

I've just been tempted to attempt (tempted to attempt? Is that good English? Well, I don't know. Is it? Isn't it? Do I look like a man who really gives a toss? Well then. If it's alright with you, I'd like to get on, as there is a telly over in the corner with my name on it) to insert a picture without first consulting the instructions that, as yet, have been a complete waste of time my bringing. I thought we'd already established that any pictures would be included at the end of this amazing piece of work......... if I've got time.........and if I can remember where I put the instructions.........and if this darn machine will let me.........and if I can be bothered.........unless there's an R in the month......... or it's raining.

Oh, shut up! You're giving me brain damage.

Oh, I'm sorry folks. Although I've got some really interesting material for you, right now, I just don't want to do this. I need an FVC.

We'll continue this intellectually stimulating conversation in the morning. And don't be late.

6:30am. Though I first woke at around 5:30am, for the next 30 minutes or so I drifted in and out of that state of not knowing whether one is awake or asleep. Frustrating, really. However, at 6:00am on the dot (I looked at my clock) I was roused from my comatose state (or should that be, rudely awakened?) by the sound of at least two patrol cars (sirens blaring) as they raced to yet another incident. Though what it was, I could not say.

At 6:15am, a helicopter arrived. *'Far too early for a trip over the Grand Canyon'*, I thought.

I pulled the curtain to one side, and peered out. Unfortunately, my view was obstructed by the veranda above, and the three floors of rooms on the opposite side of the pool. But what did it matter? What would I have seen, had my view not been obstructed? It was a police helicopter, of that there was no doubt.

Someone's been up to no good.

For all its wealth and glamour and glitz (and many would say, the perfect holiday destination), Las Vegas is no different from any other big city. Now, though I can't throw any statistics at you on this particular subject, I imagine it is no more violent, nor has any more problems with drugs and prostitution than any other American city. *'It's just another day in paradise'*. As Phil Collins so rightly said.

I left the motel at around 3:00pm yesterday, crossed the street, walked two hundred yards or so and waited patiently for the bus.

The bus being, *'The Deuce'*.

The Deuce travels up and down the strip (Las Vegas Boulevard), from north to south and south to north, 24 hours a day and costs $3 for one trip or $7 for a 24 hour pass, which can be used on any bus in Vegas. The bus arrived (I believe they run at seven minute intervals), I paid my $7 and headed south, uptown, towards Caesar's Palace.

But why Caesar's Palace? Why not any of the other casinos? The only answer I can give, is that as it was the first casino I ever gambled at (played the slots), perhaps (misguidedly) I believed that I should stay loyal. But wait! I do think (architecturally) that it is by far the finest looking hotel in Vegas. *'Yeah! Like that's going to improve my chances of striking it rich.'*

Two years ago, the Frontier hotel and casino was closed and awaiting demolition. Today, it is nothing more than a wasteland, awaiting the arrival of yet another money-making monstrosity.

On my first visit to Vegas (2001) I had a budget of $300 per day, to spend on the slots. On a bad day, it could be gone in as little as one hour, while on a good day, it might last as long as four hours. But, once it was gone, that was it. There was none of this, *'Oh, I'll just put in another ten, and another, and another'.* No. When it was gone, it was gone, and I'd spend the rest of the day simply wandering around, drinking in the majestic splendour that is, *'Las Vegas'.*

In that climate controlled twilight zone that is Caesar's Palace, I felt out of place, even overdressed. All the other male tourists wore shorts and tee shirts, or casual slacks and cotton shirts, and there was I, with my leather jacket, afraid to take it off, lest I put it down somewhere and wander off without it.

From time to time, I'd stop, take out my notebook and pen and make a note of what I saw or heard.

I began to wonder whether the CCTV controllers were observing me, and were perhaps a little suspicious of my behaviour. Maybe they were thinking, *'He could be a spy for one of the other casinos.'* Or, worse still, *'a terrorist'.* No. I probably didn't even register as a tiny blip on the radar. Just as well. I mean. Can you imagine it. *'So how was your holiday, Bren?' 'How was my holiday? How was my fucking holiday? I'll tell you how it was. I got arrested, 'cos some oaf of a security guard, who worked at the casino where I was losing all my hard-earned cash, thought I looked like a fucking terrorist. Any more questions? No? Good. Now, fuck off.'* Fortunately, that was all inside my head.

Steadily moving on.

I wandered around (like a nomad in the desert) in the search of the machine I had played back in 2001. But why? I hadn't been able to find it in 2002, or 2007. They all looked the fucking same. Hell. They'd probably even rearranged the place several times since my last visit.

I eventually settled on one machine. *'Hm. This looks like a good one.'* I sat down, and made myself comfortable, before loading my machine up with a whole $20, and then pressed the button. After several presses, I heard a voice say, *"No. You're not doing it right. You won't get paid like that."* I gave her (for it was a she) my best confused look and said, *"What?" "You're only doing one play. You have to do three plays to get paid."* (Paid. Payed. Which is the correct spelling? Are they both correct?) Of course, this means using three times as much money on one spin. Although your credit goes down three times faster, the rewards are far greater. I smiled and carried on as I had been doing, in the vain hope of making my fortune. However, after having put a mere $40 into the machine, I walked away, having spent a very pleasant ten minutes. Ah. Time for a wander.

'Java Coffee', the sign read. Yes. I'm sure it is. But the price, no doubt (though I did not see it), was probably astronomical. I passed.

'Palace Court Slots'. Here, the machines take $100 bills. I walked in. I walked out. Hey! I'm just a postman. They don't pay *me* Hollywood wages.

At a bar sat several guys. They were drinking beer, watching a ball game, while simultaneously playing the machines. *'Who said men can't multitask?'* I have to admit, I was envious. Ah. But the days when I could have spent every day of my holiday doing that, sadly, are long gone. But why do I say *sadly*? After all, the drinking *did* nearly kill me. And yet, I have so many fond memories of those times long ago. In my mind, I still see the faces of those I drank with. Unfortunately, unlike me, not all of them lived to tell the tale, so to speak. Then again, there are those who, though still alive, continue to drink (some, to excess), consequently, we no longer keep in touch. Oh, sure. I miss those days, and the people, but I could never go back.

Over at *'Pussy Cat Dolls'*, the music was annoyingly loud, though the customers seemed oblivious to it. Though I could not see them from the waist down, the croupiers (women, of course) who dealt Blackjack, wore bejewelled basques and pink caps with black patent leather peaks, which were adorned with gold anchor cap badges. Nice! Sexist? Maybe. But who's fucking holiday is this?

No. Blackjack's not for me. The pretty ladies, on the other hand. Ah, well. I can dream.

Fortunately, I had with me my shiny, new, digital camera, on which to capture every last moment of that tacky experience. Am I a cynical old sod? You bet I am.

Still. *"When in Rome.........",* as they say. After all, this *was* Caesar's Palace, was it not?

I contemplated eating at Planet Hollywood, but as there were no prices on the menu outside, I decided against it.

I wandered into one of the many gift shops, with its overpriced souvenirs, and even considered purchasing another Zippo for my collection, but walked away thinking to myself, *'I can always come back tomorrow'.*

Were the souvenir shops suffering, due to the recession? One shop I visited (selling jewellery, watches, leather belts, etcetera) had massive discounts. However, in my humble opinion, the prices were still excessive. Needless to say, after giving every item in the shop several coats of looking at, I walked away empty-handed, but with a very serious expression on my face.

Though it was only 5:15pm when I left Caesar's it was dark outside, and by that time I was ravenous. But where would I eat? I didn't want to eat at any of those busy diners and restaurants and cafés. I'm not like all the other tourists, you see. They all look the same and act the same. Hell! They even communicate with one another. I, on the other hand, prefer somewhere quiet, somewhere

where I can chat to the waiter, or waitress (even if I do sometimes bore them to tears).

I crossed the street, hopped on the first available *'Deuce'* (Not easy. Busy, busy, busy, at that time of day.) and headed north, downtown.

I got off the bus about three stops before I needed to, intending once again to eat at Denny's. But then, something caught my eye.

Across the street, and just before Denny's, I saw *'White Cross Drugs, Good Neighbour Pharmacy'*. An untidy looking building, I thought, though one should never judge a book by its cover. And, alongside the name, a sign read, *'Tiffany's Café'*. *'Got to be worth a look, hasn't it?'* I thought to myself.

Tiffany's is a relatively small café, and not the most upmarket, but the place did have a certain *'Je ne sais quoi'*, so it was good enough for me. Suited me to a tee, to be honest.

On the cover of the menu (apart from Tiffany's Café) were the words, *'Eat in, or take out. Open 24 hours a day, 365 days a year'*. What more could one want?

Having not eaten since breakfast, I was famished. So, I started with the chicken noodle soup and crackers, followed by the New York steak, carrots, cauliflower, broccoli, mashed potatoes and gravy. The meal also came with a bread roll and two glasses of coke. And, at $16.43, I was well chuffed. I left $20, and Tiffany's Café gets a 7½ out of 10.

Statistic: Did you know (this statistic goes back to 2001) that there are more swimming pools (per head of population) in Las Vegas, than in any other town, or city in America? Not a lot of people know that.

Should I go shooting today? I'll tell you later.

5:05pm. No. Didn't go shooting. Didn't feel like doing much of anything.

Last night, I got chatting to a guy who works at the gas station just down the road. If you remember, I was in dire need of an FVC. To be perfectly honest, I could just do with one now.

Hey! Now that's weird. From time to time (too many times, if I'm honest), things that have upset me in the past, come into my head and they just won't go away and I start sinking into depression. However, on other occasions, they make me angry and I don't sink. It is as though the anger were acting like a flotation device, preventing me from sinking. But I have no desire to be angry. Likewise, I have no desire to be depressed.

Now what was I saying, before all that came out? Was it something to do with pine furniture? Can't have been mahogany. No. Too expensive.

You see? This it what happens when you distract me. I lose my focus. Focus? Right now, I'm losing the will to live.

Ah! Yes. That was it. Tiffany's. I went back to Tiffany's for a spot of breakfast, and damn good it was too.

One pound of ground beef (in the form of a large burger), three eggs (overlight), home fries (fried potatoes), two pieces of toast and two cups of coffee. And all for $10.49. Another bargain. I was only too pleased to leave a $2 tip. And will I be dining there again tomorrow? Well, though I have no idea what life has in store for me, I'd say that it was a pretty safe bet.

On the wall behind the counter in Tiffany's, there is a sign with these few words on it. It simply says: *'Quality is Our Recipe'*. Ain't that the truth?

5:45pm. Speaking of food. I'm hungry. Should I try that Boston Pizza place? It's only a few doors away.

But I thought I might take in a movie. Now *there's* something we'd never say back in England. How the hell does one *'take in a movie'*? And yet, it makes perfect sense when I'm over here.

Should I decide to *'take in a movie'*, it's a toss-up between *'The men who stare at goats'* and *'Law abiding citizen'*. The first film is based on a true story (Oh, I do like a true story, don't you?) while the other (to me, at least) sounds interesting.

Of course, I then have to decide where I'd like to view either of these contributions to the world of cinema. As you might imagine, there's no shortage of movie theatres in *this* town. Oh no. *'You got that right'*, as my old friend Columbo would say.

I've just remembered what it was that we were talking about, before *you* so rudely interrupted me. Okay! Okay! It was all my fault. Do you feel better now? I can't help it if my brain suddenly switches from one subject to another.

I was telling you about the gas station. So, this guy at the gas station starts telling me about his time in England, whilst in the U S Airforce. During his tour of duty, he was fortunate (or should that be *unfortunate?*) to spend some time at Greenham Common, when all that trouble over Cruise Missiles was going on. Yeah. He remembered seeing all the protesters. This guy (presumably during a weekend break) even visited Southport, where he ate fish and chips and even remarked on how good they were. Of course, he couldn't say exactly where he'd bought them, but it's a small world, isn't it? Well, it is if you've got a car. But, if you have to walk, then it becomes a whole lot bigger.

Caesar's Palace. Las Vegas, Nevada.

Luxor Hotel. Las Vegas, Nevada.

8:15am. Good morning, good morning. I trust you haven't been waiting long? I would have got here sooner, but I've been hellishly busy reconnecting to the Internet. Every day since I got here (and sometimes more than once a day), I find that the signal is bad, or I have lost connection and must try to connect to another network. It's such a pain. Of course, I don't *have* to be on the Internet to write my journal, but I do like to check my emails first thing in the morning.

One more day, and I'm out of here.

Perhaps I should have gone skydiving, or taken another helicopter trip over the Grand Canyon. I haven't even been shooting. Maybe later.

I passed on the movies. I decided instead to get a pizza from Boston's (with pepperoni and mushrooms), a French vanilla coffee from the gas station and have a relaxing evening in front of the box. With a brand new episode of that excellent television show, *'House'*, I was happy as a sandboy. What? I have absolutely no idea what a sandboy is. Would someone kindly explain?

I was rudely awakened at 1:35am when the phone rang, though as the caller did not speak, I can only assume that whoever it was simply got the wrong number.

Yesterday was spent (once again) wandering around Caesar's Palace, although I did also have a look inside the Bellagio. But once you've seen the inside of one casino, you've seen them all. I didn't even have a go on the slots.

I must admit, I was (in my lonely state) more than a little tempted to get on the phone and order up one of those ever-so-nice-ladies. You know the ones. They come to your room, and dance for you (as it is referred to). But, at around $200 a pop, I decided against it and carried on chomping away on my pizza.

If you're ever around this way, Boston's does a pretty good pizza.

New Developments. I took photos of a couple of new developments yesterday, though I couldn't remember quite what they were replacing. There's *always* something being knocked down and *always* something being built, here in Vegas.

'*New York*'. The city that never sleeps.

'*Las Vegas*'. The city that's never *quite* satisfied with its appearance.

Struggling! Struggling! Yep. I'm struggling today folks. I'm finding it hard to come up with anything new to say. But, I guess that was inevitable. It certainly isn't worth worrying about.

'*The sun is out, the sky is blue, there's not a cloud to spoil the view......*' Hey! I could write a song about that. Oh no. Wait a minute. Damn. Buddy Holly got there first. Never mind. Perhaps it's time I did some more work on that poem about the Crazy Horse Memorial. No. I don't feel up to it.

12 noon. I've had breakfast, bought a souvenir for a good friend of mine (that would be Boz) and I've just sent two emails. My, my. I *have* been busy this morning.

Initially, I walked straight past Tiffany's Café, thinking that I might just see if the breakfast at Denny's was as good as the dinner I'd had on Saturday evening. But, I ended up walking straight past that too. So where was I going? I had no idea. I was just walking. I told myself that it was good for me, I was getting some exercise. And maybe there was some truth in that. After all, my waistline has (as it always does when I'm on holiday) expanded somewhat.

Though not *quite* as hot as the clear blue skies and brilliant sunshine suggested it might be, it was, nevertheless, warm enough to venture out without a jacket.

I walked south for about half a mile, past the Stratosphere Tower and stopped at '*Bonanza*', which is located at the corner of Sahara Avenue and Las Vegas Boulevard and where I purchased a baseball cap for Boz. Boz (Malcolm Dean. Though no one ever calls him that.) is what I would call, '*a true friend*', and there aren't many of them around. Though he himself has never visited America, nevertheless, he has acquired some knowledge of this fine country, due to the vast amount of postcards I have sent him over the years. Now then. Here's an interesting piece of trivia for you. Back in the seventies (sadly I don't know what year it was exactly) Boz was the security man for Richard and Karen Carpenter, when they were performing in Southport. Well, they do say you learn something new every day.

Here's another piece of trivia for you. Apparently, *Bonanza* is the largest gift shop in the world. Well, that's what it says on the sign. Don't shoot me, I'm just the messenger.

Every once in a while, I'll see something that I think will suit someone, and this just happened to be one of those times.

Boz *does* enjoy a game of cards. So, when I saw this cap, with the words '*Las Vegas*', and a couple of playing cards on it, I just couldn't resist it. I simply *had* to buy it. He'll get a kick out of that.

I did contemplate buying a new Zippo lighter for my collection, but managed to resist the temptation. Having said that, I would like to increase my collection. So, at some point (and I'd better make it soon), I suspect I will purchase a couple.

There wasn't anything else that took my fancy, so I did an about-turn and headed back in the direction of my motel, still agonizing over where I should eat breakfast. Would it be Denny's, or would it be Tiffany's?

I came across Denny's first, but decided against it. No. I was being drawn back to Tiffany's. Okay. Maybe it's not quite as smart as Denny's, but it's homely, relaxed, the kind of place in which one can truly feel at ease, and the food is really good too. As the sign says: '*Quality Is Our Recipe*'. And that, my friends, says it all.

As I walked in, I was greeted by the smiling face of a lady, whose name (I would later learn) was Elaine. It's so nice when people recognise you, even though they've only seen you once before.

As I studied the menu (wondering if I should try something different), I got stuck into my first coffee of the day. Good coffee it was too, just like the day before. A really good cup of coffee is as good as a fine meal. Of course, that's just my opinion.

Omelettes! Yes. I'll try an omelette. Spanish, I think. And with home fries, toast and yet more coffee, I have to say, another excellent breakfast. Price? $9.73, plus a $2 tip.

As I sat there, elbows resting on the counter, coffee mug held tightly in both hands and staring into space, *'Dancing in the dark'*, by Bruce Springsteen came on the radio. Elaine (though I still didn't know her name at that time) spoke. *"This reminds me of the eighties."* she said. *"Yes. 1984, I think."* was my reply. We spoke for a little while about the merits of the conventional juke box, and concluded that it was far superior to that of its counterpart, the video juke box.

1. You get a lot more songs for your money.

2. You can enjoy a conversation with someone, without being distracted by the video screen.

You see, if the radio is on, or a conventional juke box is playing, you don't feel a compulsion to stare at it. Whereas, if the telly is on (or there is a video screen in close proximity), then, for some reason or other, we feel compelled to stare at it. It's almost as though they exert some kind of hypnotic power over us. It doesn't matter how hard we try, *'resistance is futile'* (as *'The Borg'* would say on Star Trek).

As I was leaving Tiffany's, I struck up a conversation with Elaine. (Did she initiate the conversation, or did I? Damned if I know now.) Anyway, I told her a little about my road trips, and she asked if (when I got home) I'd send her a postcard. I said yes, and went on to say, that I'd even send her a copy of my journal, once it was printed out. So. Now, I can't wait to get it finished and send her a copy and then, wait to hear what comments, or criticisms she has to make. *'Constructive criticism is a good thing. Insults are not.'* I've just come up with that. What do you think?

There will be many more people reading this journal-cum-piece-of-junk, so, no doubt, there will be plenty of questions for me to answer.

'Excuse me. But, do you mind if I ask you a question?' 'No. Of course not. Just don't expect an answer, that's all.' Don't you just love a bit of silly humour?

Ah! Now then. That reminds me. Well, when I say *"that reminds me"*, what I mean is, that I've just seen a photo on the side of my computer that reminded me of something I was going to mention.

If you remember, last night I thought about going to see a movie, but couldn't decide, (a) whether to go, or (b) what to see. Obviously, as you now know, I didn't bother. But, the point I'm struggling to make here, is this: whilst looking through the list of movie theatres (of which there are many), I couldn't find the one next to the Fremont Street Experience, which is an arcade on Fremont Street. As it was not in the listings, I could only conclude that the theatre must have been shut down. I've seen several films there on previous visits to Vegas, but there were never all that many people in the theatre. Maybe it just wasn't paying its way.

The sun's gone in. In fact, if I'm not mistaken, the sky is turning a rather menacing shade of grey. They did say (on the weather channel) that the weather would turn bad towards the end of the week. Oh! A little hint of sun just peeped through.

2:35pm. How long have I been at this? *'Too long. And it's starting to get a little boring'* was the cry. Yeah. Like I care. You'll read it and like it, or you won't get any pudding. Now where was I?

'Ah! Reprieve. He's off to check his emails.' I hear you cry. No. Not so much a reprieve, as a stay of execution. For, as *'Arnie'* once said, *'I'll be back'*.

8:20pm. I went to the movies this evening. I saw *'Law Abiding Citizen'*. And, as I suspected, a guy is wronged and takes his revenge. It's a little more complicated than that, so I'll say no more, just in case you want to watch it. But I will say this............ No. I'm only joking.

I thought I'd take a short-cut to the movie theatre, which, coincidentally, is called Brenden Theatre. (It's nothing to do with me. It's not even spelt the same.) Unfortunately, my short cut turned out to be a *'long-cut'*. And would they let me in for half price when I told them my name? *Would they? Would they?* Would they hell as like. Anyway. It was only $5 to see the movie. The food on the other hand (two soft pretzels and a bottle of lemon and lime), cost $11.50. Daylight robbery. Robbery of the daylight variety.

After parking the car round the back of the motel, I headed off to the gas station for a paper and an FVC.

All in all, it's not been a bad day.

Hey! I made a new friend, didn't I? Elaine, at Tiffany's Café.

Damned if I know why people want to talk to me. I don't want to talk to me. But, as I spend so much time alone, I'm forced to.

Wednesday November 11th

8:45am. Well, it's my last day in Vegas. How would I describe my four days here? Were they good, bad or somewhere in-between? It's so hard to say.

However, after leaving the Palms Hotel last night (where I saw the movie *Law Abiding Citizen*), and taking that slow, slow drive home along Las Vegas Boulevard, I saw the city that I had come to despise in a totally different light.

I remember once telling a friend how totally bowled over I was the first time I visited this city.

Going into those fine buildings, with their marble, crystal and plush carpet interiors, their amazing artworks and sculptures, the sheer scale of it all was like being in the presence of some superior force. Initially, it was quite humbling.

Even on my second visit, I felt as though this was the place to be.

But, by the time of my third visit (some five years later), the veneer had worn off, you might say.

I once described the experience of walking into one of the hotels for the first time, as being like that of a child's first visit to a sweet shop. The eyes widen, the jaw drops and you just want to grab everything.

Now, I may be a cynic, and I know that I've said this on more than one occasion, but! For me, Vegas is like candy: *'Too much of it will make you sick'*.

I should at this point like to make it perfectly clear, that my views on the hotels, casinos and shopping centres, in no way reflect my views on the people of this city. Quite the contrary. I have been shown nothing but kindness by all those I have encountered.

But, what if I've been getting it wrong?

2001 and 2002 were pretty good years. And, although my 2007 road trip was not ruined by my depression (as was the case in 2006), I did, nevertheless, experience a decrease in my levels

178

of happiness from time to time. Could this have played a part in my becoming disillusioned with Las Vegas? Quite possibly. After all, I wouldn't describe myself as being on *top form* on this trip. Although I have not experienced any *deep* depressions thus far, I have felt myself sinking on more than one occasion.

Anyway, to get back to what I was saying. After trying to convince my friend how wonderful Las Vegas was, she said to me, *"Yeah. It's alright. But, once you've seen the inside of one casino and hotel, you've seen them all."* And, do you know something? She's quite right. Only the exteriors are different. Which brings us back to the beginning.

The drive home last night really was quite special.

I'm terribly sorry, but I'm going to have to cut off at this point, as it's 9:40am, I need to finish packing, have breakfast and be out of here by 11:00am. Please excuse me.

2:20pm.

It's just so annoying when you have to cut off like that. I mean, what was I going to say next?

Now, what's this rubbish I've scribbled down here? $10? The Palms? What the hell? Ah! Wait a minute. I've got it. But before I go on, a word of advice. *When making notes, just make sure that they are specific, as, the odd word (or number) could refer to absolutely anything.*

So then. $10 and The Palms. I've got it.

In a recent email from Trish (you remember Trish, don't you? Crazy woman? Lives in Lubbock, Texas? Talks a lot? Yes, that's the one), she wrote (after hearing that I was feeling a little down) *'Cheer up, Brendan. You're in Vegas. Put a quarter in a machine for me, and win big.'* So, after the movie finished, and I was walking through the casino in the Palms Hotel, I thought, *'what the hell, why not put the whole $10 in, and win some for myself as well.'* It was fantastic. I won. I lost. I lost. I won.........and then.........I lost. Still. It was only $10. Anyway, had I walked away without putting so much as a quarter in, then I probably would have gone home thinking to myself, *'what if'*. So, at least I left knowing that

I'd tried. As they say, *'It is better to try and fail, than not to try at all'*. Does anyone actually believe that shit? Oh no! Mr Cynical just got home.

Will I ever return to Vegas?

I told Trudy that I'd take her there, if she wanted me to.

Elaine said, *"Come back and see us sometime."* And I replied, *"I'll make a point of coming back next year."* But would I be happy? Oh. Life can be so confusing.

Hey! Did I tell you that I got talking to a postman the other day? Yeah. He said that they'd remodelled Econo Lodge. Oh. You remember. The motel I stayed at in 2001, 2002 and again in 2007, where the carpet in my room still had that same stain after six years. Well. I may miss out on my Wyndham Rewards Points, but it might just be worth checking it out. That's if I *do* come back next year.

Maybe the only way I could ever *really* enjoy Vegas, is if I were wealthy.

In which case, that's precisely what I choose to be. Wealthy. Bring it on.

I had my final breakfast in Tiffany's this morning. Three eggs (overlight), corned beef hash, home fries, toast and three cups of coffee. $9.60, plus a $2 tip.

Elaine wasn't there. Though she had said (only the day before) that she might not be.

Once again, I started off telling you about something, only to get sidetracked.

So, there I was, heading east on Flamingo Road, slowly making my way through the heavy traffic towards Las Vegas Boulevard (having just seen a pretty good movie), when it hit me. (Not literally, of course.) It was beautiful. It was magnificent. It was Christmas on the biggest movie screen in the world.

Though artificial, it gave me that same sense of wonder I had felt when first I gazed out across the Painted Desert, and observed the artistry of Mother Nature herself.

This was (by far) the most spectacular light show one could imagine.

These architectural wonders of the modern world, though nothing more than concrete, steel and glass, took on almost lifelike form when illuminated by a million coloured lights that flickered and danced and entertained me as I made my way home.

I had no interest in the magicians, the singers, the comedians, or any of the other performers. For me, *'this'* was the greatest show in 'Las Vegas'. For this, I could quite easily return to Vegas. It gave me a buzz, a high, it was like nothing I had ever seen, or could ever hope to see if I lived to be a thousand. I was in awe of this truly amazing sight.

This was man competing with nature. And, though coming a close second, nevertheless, a very commendable performance, in my opinion.

Of course, this makes it the perfect place for lovers. Be they married, engaged, or just dating, what could be more romantic than a stroll down Las Vegas Boulevard after dark?

I feel quite exhausted after all that. I really don't know where I get it from some days.

Though it's only 4:45pm, the sun is setting and the darkness is descending.

Better think about getting something to eat.

When I checked in, the lady at reception informed me that if I showed my key card at Denny's, I'd get 10% off my meal. Isn't life just wonderful? (Do you think I should add the word *sometimes* to that last sentence, hm?) There's that negativity creeping in again. It's forever raising its ugly head. Been the bane of my life, it has. The bane of my life, and no mistake.

Anyone for Denny's? No? Suit yourself. I'll see you later. Okay?

9:00pm. Denny's. Needles, California.

Not bad. I started with the beef and veg soup, with plenty of crackers. Then I moved onto the *'Chicken Sizzler'*, chargrilled chicken, sautéed onion and peppers, hash browns topped with cheese and bacon, garlic bread, sour cream and salsa.

The menu said that the dish came with tortilla wraps, but I was given garlic bread. So, instead of an 8, Denny's is downgraded to a 7. An elementary mistake. Should I have said something? Yeah. Probably.

Don't get me wrong. The meal was delicious. It's just a shame they got it wrong.

I really should have done this when I got back from dinner at 6:00pm.

No. Sorry. It's no good. I'll see if I can give a more detailed account in the morning.

THURSDAY NOVEMBER 12TH

7:20am. Needles, California. Though small (the town has a population of no more than 6000), the Internet connection here is far better than that of Las Vegas. Too much fannying about there.

After checking out of my Vegas motel, I drove north for a couple of blocks, then east on Charleston Boulevard for about three miles, joined Interstate 515 (which becomes the 93/95) and headed south towards Highway 95.

I drove for several miles before reaching a fork in the road. The left fork was the 93, which heads east towards the Hoover Dam, before crossing the state line and on into Arizona. That is a route I have taken on many occasions, travelling both east and west. The right fork (Highway 95, and a road I was unfamiliar with) heads south, towards California.

As I joined this new route, before me lay what can only be described as a barren wilderness, scarred by power lines, one major highway and a few dirt tracks.

In the distance and over to my right, I could see what appeared to be a salt flat. As I drew closer, I saw motorbikes, quad bikes and even cars, whose drivers were *probably* competing against each other for the coveted trophy of *'King of the Idiots'*. Still. Heigh ho. That's life.

After some 60 miles I pulled into the tiny town of Searchlight, intent on filling the tank. However, when I saw the price of the gas ($2.89 per gallon. Monstrous), I decided to settle for $10 worth. And to think, I could have got it for a mere $2.59 in Vegas.

I can only assume that the salt flat was once an inland sea that had dried up hundreds of thousands (if not millions) of years ago. *'Well! How very perceptive, Sherlock.' 'Ah! Sedimentary, my dear Watson. Sedimentary.'*

Signs commemorating military conflicts were dotted along Highway 95.

There were six, if I remember rightly: *'Dedicated to the veterans of World War One, World War Two, The Korean War, The Vietnam War, The Gulf War and The War on Terrorism'.*

I took advantage of the 10% discount at Denny's and paid only $13.57 for my meal. I left the waitress a $2.50 tip, then headed down to the nearest gas station for an FVC. $1.69. Cheap. Ah! Bisto. No. Sorry. What I meant to say was, 'Ah! Luxury'.

I got onto the Internet last night and booked my accommodation for this evening. I'm getting quite good at this Internet lark, aren't I?

I shall be staying in Gallup, New Mexico. And the price will be……erm……let me see, let me see……Ah! Here it is. $52.16. And that includes the tax.

I *had* thought about staying in Holbrook, Arizona once again, simply so that I could pay another visit to the Painted Desert, but then I decided that it would keep for another road trip.

I slept badly last night, because it was too damn hot. I could, of course, have put the air conditioning on, but then the noise would have kept me awake. I guess it must have got a little cooler in the early hours of the morning, as I did get *some* sleep.

Heading back east I'll lose an hour every time I cross a time zone, one of which is a mere 5 miles from here, when I cross the state line into Arizona.

I estimate Gallup to be about 400 miles from here. So. Providing there's a tail wind, the geese are flying south for the winter, and there's also a bright golden haze on the meadow……
…I can expect to be there at around 4:30pm. Of course, that's if I leave here at 10:00am.

9:05am. I had breakfast a couple of hours ago. Free. Nothing special. Just Raisin Bran, a toasted bagel with cream cheese and two cups of coffee.

6:55pm. Days Inn, Gallup, New Mexico. (Finally.)

Although initially I did go to the wrong Days Inn (Yes! There are two in Gallup. But then I already knew that) I did eventually make it to the right one (about an hour later). *'Nothing wrong in that'*, you say.

Well, no. Technically there isn't. But listen, while I tell you a cautionary tale.

Travel east on Interstate 40, leave it at exit 16 and there, at 3201 West Highway 66, you'll find a Days Inn motel. Unfortunately, this is not the Days Inn you require. Oh, no. *You* will be wanting the Days Inn that is located about 2½ miles from exit 20, once you have left the interstate.

So, having left the interstate at the correct exit, you *assume* (wrongly, of course) that the motel must be on the straight road on which you are travelling. (Wrong again, Einstein.) After driving for approximately 4 miles and having not reached your destination, needless to say, you start to get a little angry. So. You pull off the road (into someone's driveway) and check the motel book for directions. *'Ah! Now then,'* you say to yourself. *'When I came off the interstate at exit 20, I was supposed to head south on Highway 602, turn right onto Aztec and see the sign for Route 66.'* So now, what you must do, is go back the way you came. However, as you are now going in the opposite direction, you must turn left onto Aztec (not right) and *then* follow Route 66. All well and good. But, now you have another problem. Where are the signs for Route 66? Perhaps they've been stolen. Nothing new there.

Eventually (after stopping to ask for directions), you discover (to your dismay), that you have been directed to the Days Inn motel just off exit 16. AAAAARGH. You might well scream.

But let's backtrack a second. I'd like you to take the time (if you would be so kind) to look once again at the address of this motel. Yes. You'll find it close to the top of the page. Have you read it? Oh, goodie. Well now I can give you the address of the Days Inn motel located close to exit 20. It is as follows: 1603 West Highway 66. Yes, folks. They're less than 3 miles apart, and.........and.........and.........you guessed it. *'THEY'RE ON THE SAME FUCKING ROAD!'*

For *'Highway 66'*, read Route 66.

What is the fucking point in sending people to exit 20, from which you cannot instantly access Route 66, when all they have to do is tell them to leave the interstate at exit 16 and, should the first Days Inn be full, then there's another one just down the road. *Swear? Swear?* I was ready to kill someone, anyone, even myself.

It's alright. You can come out from behind the sofa now. I've calmed down a little.

So. What else happened today?

I've just had dinner at the Mexican restaurant next door. *'Garcia's Sunset Grill'.* Specializing in Mexican and American Food. Owned by Carlos and Dora Garcia.

It's similar to that Mexican place I dined at in Clinton, Oklahoma. No. Sorry. Can't remember the name of it offhand.

I had the combo burritos (I *think* it contained beef and chicken) with rice, beans and salad, a bowl of tortilla chips with chilli sauce and a coke. Not bad. $11.82 for the meal, plus a $2 tip, and a final score of 7/10.

Although Garcia's does serve breakfast, lunch and dinner, I'll probably just have the free breakfast here.

I picked up a free newspaper in the lobby, so I'll just have a look-see what's on the box. And with that, he was gone. But would he return? Does anyone know? Does anyone really give a shit?

Howard Johnson Inn. Las Vegas, Nevada.

Shalimar Wedding Chapel, inside the Howard Johnson Inn.

FRIDAY NOVEMBER 13TH

8:40am. Eric Burden and the Animals.

Whilst feasting on Raisin Bran, banana and my usual two cups of coffee, the song: *'House of the rising sun'* came on the radio, and jogged a memory.

Now, I'm fairly sure I haven't already told you this, and if I have, well, what can I say?

Though I can't tell you whether I was on the 515, the 215, or the 15, I do know that I was somewhere in the Las Vegas area when I saw a sign on one of the hotels that was promoting Eric Burden and the Animals. Now, although *you* might not find that snippet of information all that interesting, I do, as I thought they'd disappeared off the radar decades ago.

On the subject of music. I was so glad to be back on the road again, as I *finally* managed to locate *'KZKE Route 66 good time oldies'*, albeit briefly. Oh, no. I had listened to no more than a dozen songs, when the radio began to crackle and the sounds of the sixties were gone. Tragic.

Still. Mustn't grumble. I did get to hear some great tracks. I should point out, that not all of these songs were from the Route 66 channel, which incidentally, is broadcast from both Seligman and Kingman, Arizona.

Every breath you take: The Police.

Eight days a week: The Beatles.

The things we do for love: 10 cc.

Without you: Harry Nilsson. (what an amazing song)

Born to be wild: Steppenwolf.

Slow Dancing: Johnny Rivers. (1978. I remember taping this song, along with a lot of others, when I was working on that fire-fighting ship in the North Sea. Hm. Might still have that tape, somewhere)

Ruby Tuesday: The Rolling Stones.

You wear it well: Rod Stewart. (This reminds me of someone special. But we won't go into that.)

Pleasant Valley Sunday: The Monkees.

Summer in the city: But I don't know who sang it. (Big Al would know.)

Goodbye Yellow Brick Road: Elton John.

Get Back: The Beatles.

Love grows where my Rosemary goes: Again. I don't know who sang it.

Your Song: Elton John.

Oh, what a night: Frankie Valli and the Four Seasons.

I love rock and roll: Joan Jett and the Black Hearts. (Though I would stop short of saying that I was a fan of Joan Jett, as this is one of Hannah's favourite songs, I thought I'd include it.)

I have no idea where I shall be spending tonight. But! I just hope it's quieter than this place. Oh, don't get me wrong. This is a good motel, compared to some I've had the misfortune to stay at. No. The problem is not the motel, it's those blasted trains. The railway line is a mere 200 yards from here, and trains rumbles through town every hour. Yes. Even through the night. Now, that wouldn't be too bad. I could get used to that. But they will insist on blowing their horns every time they come through. Yes. Even at night. So, by the time the 3:00am train turned up, I just couldn't get back to sleep.

Should I try to make it back to Amarillo?

I could have dinner at the Big Texan again. Maybe there'll be another *'crazy'*, attempting to eat the 72 ounce steak.

No. I fancy somewhere quieter.

What about going back to Tucumcari? Yeah. It's only about 350 miles from here. I could check-out of here at 11:00am, and be there by 4:00pm.

4:30pm. Tucumcari, New Mexico.

Yep. I made it. No slip-ups. Though I almost had a head-on collision with a rather large truck.

It was 20 miles east of Gallup and I was attempting to make a left turn into a gas station. A woman who was coming out had her car too far forward, thus causing me to keep my eye on her and not on the truck coming in my direction. Though I had the right of way over her, the truck had the right of way over me. We were on a collision course. I braked hard and stopped. He braked hard and swerved. I felt certain both vehicles would collide. Fortunately, they didn't. I reversed, raised my hands in apology and we all carried on, no harm done. Was someone watching over me? I guess so.

I've driven 310 miles today, with just that one stop for gas. Yes. I know. It's not a lot.

Amarillo is only two hour's drive from here, but with that hour to add on, for me it was a bridge too far.

I'm staying at a Microtel. My second of the trip. Now why did I think that I'd already written that once today? Is it *'Deja vu'?* No. I've just remembered. I put it in an email to Trish.

This motel is a little strange. No. Strange isn't the right word, is it?

What I mean is, prior to leaving Gallup, I got on the Internet to make a reservation for my stay at this motel. However, *'Computer said no'* (Little Britain). But seriously. When I tried to make a reservation, they had no rooms available. For reasons unknown, I turned up anyway and, not only did they have a room, they had a room on the first floor, which saved me having to lug my gear up to one of the upper floors. Yes. I do prefer a room on the first floor. For those of you with short memories: for first floor, read ground floor. Okay?

Though similar to the room I was given at the Microtel in Delphos, Ohio, something about it is different, though I can't quite put my finger on what. It'll come to me.

The room is $62.40 per night, as opposed to the $71.99 that I paid in Delphos.

Another difference between here and Delphos, is that I *won't* be dining in a bar this evening. Speaking of dining. I'm starving.

Thus far, it's been a pretty uneventful day. No! That's not what I mean. Yes. I did nearly get flattened by a *'Big Rig'*, but *apart* from that, there's nothing else to report.

Oh! I just remembered something. There were two cars in the middle two lanes of Interstate 40 as I was going through Albuquerque, that had been involved in a collision. Though I didn't actually see the crash, it appeared to me (due to the location of the vehicles), that one had pulled in front of the other, and the second car had rear-ended the first. The problem (as I'm sure you're all aware) is that some drivers switch lanes so often (and usually without first checking their mirrors) that it's inevitable.

Why! Even I've nearly side-swiped a few vehicles in my time. Having said that, I do *try* to be careful.

7:30pm. I've just had dinner at *'Del's Restaurant'* and, as it happens, it's not the first time I've eaten there. But just let me check my records, and I'll tell you *exactly* when that last time was.

Yes. It was Saturday October 13th 2007. I was driving a Black Chevrolet Cobalt, with 3001 miles on the clock. (I'm not making this up. It's all in my records.) But don't you *dare* ask me what the licence plate number was. I'm good, but I'm not that good.

Back then, I stayed at Motel 6, and I paid a mere $35.77 for the night. You see? It pays to keep records. It's how I've managed to fill so many of these pages. Only joking. Just a bit of fun. I'm managing to fill so many of these pages with all the rubbish that's in my head. Of course, I *could* take it to a landfill site, but they'd probably charge me to dump it. So, on reflection, it's probably more environmentally friendly to put it all down on paper, wouldn't you say?

Hey! Do you remember me once telling you that I stayed here (Tucumcari) back in 2001? No? Well, never mind. Or was it 2002? Damn! You've got me all confused now. Well, whenever it was, back in 2007 I went looking for the motel I had stayed at several years earlier. This wasn't easy, as (a) I never knew the name of the place and, (b) I'd only seen it in the dark. So, it wasn't such a good idea to go looking for it in the daylight. Needless to say, I didn't find it. However, whilst on my way to Del's Restaurant (which was recommended to me by the lady at reception), I spied something with my little eye and I'm 95% certain that it was in fact The Safari Motel that I stayed at all those years ago. But, back then, I was a novice. It was dark, I saw the word motel, and like a moth to a flame, I was drawn to it.

Now, however, things are different. I'm an old hand, a seasoned professional, a road tripper extraordinaire. *'Yep. That's me alright.'* he said, as he spilt his FVC down the front of his tee shirt. Never mind. I need to do some laundry anyway.

There's another thing about the last time I was in this town. I was here a month earlier than this (in 2007) and yet, the *'Blue Swallow Motel'* was closed for the season. Is it closed now? No. Does it have any vacancies? Yes.

When last I saw the Blue Swallow, I remember thinking that it looked like a bit of a dive. But when I remember some of the atrocious abodes I've had the misfortune to stay in, I think to myself, *'there's just no way it could be as bad as them.'* Plus! If it was good enough for Elvis, then it's good enough for me. Yes. I seem to recall reading somewhere that Elvis himself once stayed at the *Blue Swallow.*

I know. When I get home, I shall check the place out on the Internet, and the next time I'm around this way, I'll phone up (or get online) and make a reservation. Yeah. *'The job's a good-un.'*

So. *Del's Restaurant.* The menu is not as extensive as it was in 2007. Maybe they change it when things start to get a little quiet, when it's mainly the smaller number of locals who eat there, rather than the *'shedloads'* of tourists they can expect to get in the summer. Yeah. That's logical.

Having not eaten a steak in……oh……let me see…...two days?……three days? I plumped for the 12 ounce Rib-eye. This was served with a knob of parsley butter, mushrooms and pilaf rice. And I was allowed to help myself to as much soup and salad as I could manage.

The steak, though tender, had far too much fat on it. I would even go so far as to say that one third of my steak was fat.

Though overall the meal was good, instead of what should have been an 8, *Del's Restaurant* only gets a 7/10.

I had a sweet iced tea with my meal (now there's a change), and the bill came to $20.23, plus a $3 tip.

After my meal, I went for a walk up to the Blue Swallow and took a few pictures. I may take a few more in the morning.

8:55pm. All I've got to do now is the music. No. You can wait 'til tomorrow.

Brendan J. A. O'Leary

Friends Inn. Tucumcari, New Mexico. I stayed here in 2001.

The Blue Swallow Motel. Tucumcari, New Mexico.

Saturday November 14th

7:45am. Early, today.

This is quite an amazing motel. They have a heated indoor swimming pool (and spa), a fitness centre (though I haven't as yet located it), free local *and* long distance calls (within the USA, of course) and a hot breakfast.

After my usual Raisin Bran, I had a sausage and egg sandwich and two cups of coffee. I've often been tempted to make myself one of those large waffles but, as yet, I haven't plucked up the courage to attempt it.

Unfortunately, there is always a downside. In my case, I can get no signal on my phone. Thank God for emails.

I retired to bed a little after 11:00pm, but two hours later I woke to find myself absolutely dripping with sweat. But why? It wasn't particularly hot. Was it something I had eaten?

Fortunately, I always bring a large bath towel with me. This I placed on top of the bottom sheet, pulled the top sheet and the blanket over it, flipped the pillow over and, after drying myself off, spent the rest of the night under the counterpane.

The next five hours were pretty restless. I was woken by the slightest sound. The motor from the fridge in the room next door, a drip from the tap in the bathroom (close the door, Brendan) and even the occasional passing car.

6:30am. It was no good. Though still tired, I knew that I had a busy day ahead of me, especially if I wanted to make it all the way to Fort Smith, Arkansas, which, at a *guesstimate,* is about 550 miles away. But who knows. Maybe I'll stop short and find somewhere in eastern Oklahoma to lay my weary head.

I want to get some more photos of the *Blue Swallow* before I leave, and a couple of that motel I stayed at in 2001.

Now, where's that notebook? How can you lose things in a motel room? I'll swear there are spirits who move things around when my back is turned.

There's just yesterday's music to get through, and then me and my camera are off for a wander. No! You can't come with us. You know what you're like. You'll only distract me.

Mister Postman: (appropriate) The Beatles.

I go to pieces: Peter and Gordon.

Carrie Ann: The Hollies.

Miss You: The Rolling Stones.

It don't come easy: Ringo (don't call me by me stage name) Starr.

Do you remember *'Photograph'*, by Ringo Starr? That was a good song.

7:40pm. Okemah, Oklahoma.

Originally (as you know), I had planned to try and make it to Fort Smith, Arkansas, but, as that proved to be just a little too far, I then decided that I was going to settle for Sallisaw, Oklahoma, which ironically, is a mere 25 miles from Fort Smith. However, on realizing that Sallisaw was also a bridge too far (so to speak), I brought my (supposed) final destination closer still. This *was* to be Henryetta, Oklahoma. But, after checking my motel books and discovering that the only motel offering Wyndham Rewards Points was a Super 8 that I had stayed at twice in the past, I brought my final destination even closer. Phew! That wasn't easy.

Okemah is approximately 20 miles west of Henryetta, and was the birth place of the legendary Woody Guthrie, he of the, *'This land is your land, this land is my land'* fame.

Although I do know the name Woody Guthrie, I can't tell you very much about him, other than he was a folk singer and a poet. So. A bit like Bob Dylan, I guess.

I'm staying at a Days Inn, which, curiously enough, is located at 605 South Woody Guthrie Street, Okemah, Oklahoma. 74859. (In case you're interested.)

I made a mistake yesterday. I said that I'd found the motel I'd stayed at back in 2001. I told you that I'd stayed at *The Safari Motel*. But I didn't. You see, whilst on a wander this morning (taking more photos of *The Blue Swallow*), I spotted a motel that I remembered was opposite the one I did actually stay at. Back then, after checking into *my* motel, I remember seeing it (with its smart yellow sign topped by a *'triple A badge'*, American Automobile Association) and wishing I'd checked in there instead.

That particular motel (with its smart yellow sign) is called The American Motel.

Now then. Not only did I find the motel I had stayed at back then, I also spotted the establishment I ate at on that very evening, all those years ago. *'All those years ago? Try eight. It's not exactly ancient history'.*

Sadly, both the motel and the eatery are closed down. Boarded up. Derelict. Vandalized. Though I can't be sure of the name of the place I ate at (as the sign had gone), I'm fairly sure that it was *Arby's*. The motel, however, was called *'Friends Inn'*.

Next door to the motel, though also closed down, is a diner (was a diner). Did I eat breakfast there? I can't remember. I probably did. But why can't I remember?

Though I can't be certain about which room I was in, I do remember that it was towards the end of the building and on the left.

At the front of the building, the windows of the reception (where I had checked in) were boarded up. However, when I walked around the corner, I found that one small window had not been covered, which enabled me to peer in and observe that there was actually a light on inside. I tried the door handle, but it was locked. Odd, that one light should still be on. I mean. Who's going to pay the electricity bill, now that the place is *'no more'*?

I walked over to the pool (a feature I had not seen on my stay), just to see that it contained only a small amount of water and had a lot of tall grasses growing in it.

The final insult for this once proud establishment? A burnt-out van in the parking lot. Also, although I didn't know it back then, *'Friends Inn'* is actually on Route 66.

I drove the short distance down to the *Blue Swallow*, and left my car in the parking lot of yet another abandoned motel, which was just across from the *Blue Swallow*.

Apart from wanting to take a few more photos, I was hoping to have a chat with the owners and find out what they charged for the night. Sadly, the door to the office was locked and the sign read, *'Back at 3:00pm'*.

It was only after taking a couple of photos that I spotted an older woman coming out of one of the rooms. I walked over and, after explaining why I was there, she informed me that she was in fact, just the manager, and the owners (who were there from February to September) had gone back to their home in Arizona for the winter.

I told her that I had visited the motel back in October of 2007, and had seen that it was closed for the winter, which was why, on this occasion, I was so surprised to see it open in November. She informed me that although they *would* normally close, either at the end of September, or early October, as they still had bookings coming in, they'd decided to stay open for another month. *'Make hay while the sun shines'*, as they say.

SUNDAY NOVEMBER 15TH

8:40am. I'm late today. Not that it really matters. Even if I don't check out until 11:00am, and then drive for six hours, I'll still be just about where I need to be, which is anywhere just west of Memphis. From there, I'm less than three hours drive away from Dickson. Home again. If indeed there is anywhere that I can *truly* call home. But let's not go there.

Notes. Notes. Where would I be without my notes?

Now, here's a good piece of advice for you. Should you ever find yourself in my position (wandering around America and writing about your travels), then always remember to write-up the day's events on the actual day they happen (should there be anything worth writing about, of course), as if you don't, it can be hellishly difficult doing it the following day.

Obviously, even with these few notes, I'm still struggling. So. Let that be a lesson to you...... and me also.

Sheila! Yes, Sheila. That was her name (I think). She's the lady I met yesterday, at the *Blue Swallow* motel.

I felt so privileged when she let me look at one of the rooms. There are a total of 11 rooms, though I can't remember how many were singles and how many were doubles. Did she say that one of them was a suite? Yes. I think she did.

Though the room was small and simply furnished, it was nevertheless adequate. It had a bed, a television, a sink, a toilet, a shower (no room for a bath), sufficient space to store one's bits and bobs, a writing desk (if I remember rightly) and even Internet access. And! Each of the rooms had its own little garage. So, provided you didn't drive one of those large SUV's, you'd even got off-road parking.

Some of the garages were open, and I was amazed to see that the interiors had murals painted on them. The one I took a picture of was of a scene from the film *'Easy Rider'*, where Peter Fonda, Dennis Hopper and Jack Nicholson are on the motorbikes. Cool, man. Oddly enough, *'Born to be wild'* by Steppenwolf was on the radio again today. (I mean yesterday.)

The motel reminded me very much of the *Mid-Town Motel*, in Boothbay Harbour, Maine, where I was fortunate enough to stay only last year, which if I remember, was owned by a great guy called Tim Lewis.

The Mid-Town dates back to the mid-fifties, while the *Blue Swallow* was built in the late thirties.

My memory's playing tricks on me. Now, who did Sheila say had painted those murals? If I remember rightly (though don't quote me on this), I think she said that it was a guy called Jerry, who drove one of those camper vans up and down the old road, and had spent three months painting them. (Last year? The year before? I should have taken notes.) Anyway. It *could* have been Jerry McClanahan, author of EZ66, a book without which I would be totally lost. Having said that, I do still get lost from time to time.

I do know that Jerry is also an artist, and one of his paintings can be found in the lobby of the Cowboy Palace Theatre in Amarillo, Texas. Didn't somebody once write a song about that? Amarillo? Brillo? Armadillo? Bah! It's all the bloody same to me.

The price to stay at this amazing piece of history? (*The Blue Swallow*)

It's not cheap. Oh no. You'd better be prepared to raid your piggy bank, cash in your premium bonds, or use that rainy-day fund that you keep hidden under your mattress.

The lowest price is $45, plus tax. While you can expect to pay as much as, wait for it, wait for it, don't be hasty, $55, plus tax. What a bargain. Wouldn't you say?

Of course, that's what they are charging this year. Next year, the price may have increased by $5 per night, putting it well out of your price range. Who knows? Maybe you'll just have to settle for slumming it at the Hilton.

After leaving Tucumcari, I saw a sign that read: *'Amarillo. Home of the 72 ounce steak. One hour away'*. While about a hundred yards down the road, another sign read: *'Amarillo. 117 miles'*. Now. Answer me this, if you can. Unless you are travelling at 117 miles per hour, how the fuck can Amarillo be only one hour away?

Okemah is located just off Interstate 40, at exit 221. While 29 miles back (at exit 192), you'll find the town of Earlsboro. But why mention this? Simply because, from the interstate, I glimpsed a motel that I had stayed at back in 2001. I could see that it was closed down, and nature was reclaiming it (weed by weed).

Maybe I should have stopped and taken a photo of it. After all, I do have one of the time I stayed there.

Shortly before Earlsboro, there was a sign advertising the *Biscuit Hill Restaurant*, which is where I ate on the night I stayed at that now closed motel. Mm. Tender chunks of beef in a rich gravy, with mashed potatoes. I can still taste it.

Why does that time (though only eight years) seem like a lifetime ago? Eight years is nothing.

I asked the lady at reception if she could recommend somewhere where I could get a good meal in Okemah. She directed me to the *Brick Street Café*, about a mile away. As you know, I'm not keen on driving in the dark, but I did manage to find it without *too* much difficulty.

The place was large, and what I'd describe as *'warehouse-like'* inside. Apart from the main dining area, it appeared to have a basement dining area, presumably for when they got really busy. They even had several tables on the balcony above the bar, counter and kitchen areas.

The walls were covered with all manner of memorabilia. (More later.)

5:00pm. Forrest City, Arkansas. Yep. I certainly do get around.

I've just been checking my mileage. And, I'm a mere four miles short of 8,000 miles driven, thus far.

Tomorrow, I shall be back in Dickson, and this year's adventure will effectively be over. What will next year bring?

So. Getting back to the *Brick Street Café*.

Unfortunately, the place was draughty, which, as I'm sure you know by now, loses it a point. Sad. But I mustn't show any favouritism.

I started with a large basket of tortilla chips, with salsa dip. The tortilla chips were hot, which is unusual. But it proved that they were cooked to order. Then I had the fish platter. (Though it wasn't called that, I can't remember what it was called. Damn.) This was butterflied shrimp (breaded and deep fried), small pieces of catfish (breaded and deep fried), popcorn shrimp (smaller shrimp? breaded and deep fried), a spicy tomato dipping sauce and chips. With a Pepsi, the bill came to $17.73, plus a $3 tip. Not bad. I'd go there again. But! I'd make damn sure I wasn't sitting in a draught. Score? 7/10.

Music. (November 14th.)

Go your own way: Fleetwood Mac.

Hello Goodbye: The Beatles.

I cry like a baby: The Box Tops.

The Guitar Man: David Gates and Bread.

Born to be wild: Steppenwolf.

Living like a refugee: Tom Petty and the Heartbreakers.

Am I glad that not a lot has happened today! No. It's not a question. I'd say it was more of a statement. Wouldn't you?

7:40pm. I would have been back sooner, but I've just been messing about, trying to attach a photo to a document without using the instructions. Did it go? Didn't it go? I don't flaming well know. You may as well ask me what the moon's made of.

I was sending an email to Hannah, as this is where I met her only last year. Of course, she doesn't actually live here. I *believe* she's living somewhere in Memphis, though it could be Madrid for all I know.

After checking out of the motel in Okemah, I put $15 worth of gas in the tank, got onto the interstate and once again started heading east.

For about an hour, the rain came down and the visibility was low, but I didn't care. No. As it turns out, Forrest City is only a 350 mile drive from Okemah.

I'm struggling here folks. Would somebody kindly help me out?

'The well of intellectuality has run dry.' It's all gone. You've had the lot. There's nothing left of me.

Oh, my Lord. What's this? Get this. My computer has just shown me the *'tip of the day'. 'Automatic Tables Formatting'. Works has over 15 automatic table formatting options for you to select from when creating or editing your tables. 'Learn More'.* Learn more? I didn't understand the first fucking bit. No thank you, Mister Computer. I'll pass, if that's alright with you. It is? Oh, jolly dee.

Did you know that Tulsa (Oklahoma) has a Christmas radio station? No? Okay. Fair enough. But, the question is this: Do they play Christmas songs all year round? Although I came across it today (whilst trying to find a station that was playing decent music), I also managed to tune into it about three weeks ago.

Music.

Hold me now: The Thompson Twins.
Don't speak: No Doubt.
Rocket Man: Elton John.
Tumbling Dice: The Rolling Stones.
Breakfast in America: Supertramp.
The boys are back in town: Thin Lizzy.

This is no good. I'm drained. I'm like a credit card that's *maxed-out.* I'll try again tomorrow. Maybe my batteries will have recharged by then.

Wouldn't you just flaming well know it. Just as I'm about to switch off the computer, I remember a few things.

They're not all that important, but then, who decides what is or isn't important?

I paid $54.63 to stay at the Days Inn motel in Okemah, while the Days Inn here in Forrest City is costing me $69.55. To be perfectly honest, there really isn't that much difference, but there you go.

I had dinner at *Bonanza*, here in Forrest City. And before you ask. No! None of the Cartwrights were there. Can you not be serious for once? Oh, I do despair, some days.

This was my third visit to *Bonanza,* having also had the pleasure of dining there in 2007 and 2008.

I thought I'd push the boat out once again, and go for the 12 ounce Rib-eye with baked potato.

Once you have ordered your meal, and are waiting for it to be served, you simply help yourself to all the other hot and cold food at the buffet. I just had a very large plate of salad and a glass of sweet iced tea.

Though the steak wasn't up to the standard of that at La Ventana, in Grants, New Mexico, it was far better than the steak I was served in Tucumcari, New Mexico.

The meal was a mere $16.49, and I left a $3 tip.

Yep. *Bonanza* is a place I would strongly recommend for a good feed.

Bonanza gets an 8/10. Well done, and not a cowboy in sight.

MONDAY NOVEMBER 16 *TH*

8:35am. It's raining.

I've been staring at this page for the last ten minutes, and I haven't a clue what to say.

I've just been counting the business cards that I've accumulated from all the motels I've stayed at. Thus far, I've stayed at 25 different motels. By the time I've checked into the Super 8 motel in Dickson, Tennessee (later today), it will be my 26th stay, though some would say that it's *still* only 25 as I've already stayed at that particular motel once, and that was *before* I started my road trip.

I could, of course, check into another motel in Dickson, simply to avoid any discrepancies in my final tally of motel stays, but as it is such a pleasant establishment and the manager (Vince) and his family (wife, Mita and son, Jay) are such wonderful people, I wouldn't want to stay anywhere else.

Why were the words flowing so freely for so long? Is this writer's block that I am experiencing?

Once, my imagination ran riot. Now, it doesn't have the enthusiasm to get out of bed. Hey! That's not bad. We could be on a roll here. Nope. Spoke too soon. The engine has stalled again.

3:45pm. I'm back in Dickson, but I still haven't managed to come up with anything *remotely* of interest to say.

I checked in at 2:30pm and, after chatting with Vince's wife, Mita, for a while, I called Stella. Unfortunately, she's not well enough to receive visitors, so that's depressed me. However, she did say that I could call again in the morning and, God willing, if she and Orville are a little better, then it might just be alright for me to go up and see them. I really do hope that they are well enough for me to pay them a visit.

I tried calling Trudy, but, surprise surprise, her phone's switched off.

Sometimes, I wish I didn't form attachments to people. I just end up getting hurt.

8:50pm. Well, I'll tell you this, if I tell you nothing else. I may have been ever so slightly depressed earlier, but I'm not anymore. *'How so?'* I hear you cry. Well, if you really, really want to know, then I shall tell you.

It's simple.

I've just spent an hour conversing with a very interesting and intelligent woman, who is now my email penfriend. Her name's Amanda. She did (if I'm not mistaken) get a mention or two in last year's journal.

I had dinner at Farmers. Yes. That would be the all-you-can-eat place, just two doors away. I shall not bore you with the details, save-to-say, I had two large plates of dinner and two puddings, all washed down with a large glass of coke.

I *was* going to catch a movie, but as I was enjoying Amanda's company so much, I decided against it.

After leaving the *'Pay Less Shoe Source'* (which is where Amanda works), I drove back to the motel, nipped over to the gas station for an FVC and a paper, and now, as I sit here, writing nothing but rubbish, I'm wondering to myself, *'Why the hell am I doing this, when there's probably something really interesting on the telly?'*

Yep. Life's a mystery, and no mistake.

There were only two decent songs on the radio today.

Penny Lane: The Beatles.

Against all odds: Phil Collins. (My third favourite song.)

TUESDAY NOVEMBER 17TH

9:25am. Though it may appear that I am late starting work today (if indeed this could be described as work), as I am no longer up against the clock (as far as checking out is concerned), it really doesn't matter what time I start tap, tap, tapping.

Damn! I was leading up to something there, but now I've lost it. Never mind. With a bit of luck (and let's face it, at this stage, I could really use some), it'll come back to me.

Still no word from Trudy. But that's nothing new.

I'm worried about calling Stella and Orville, as I fear that once again they will not be well enough to receive visitors.

I talk to God. I ask him to watch over them, and make them well again, but I guess that He/She/It doesn't consider it a priority. Which begs the question: What's the point of all this, *'Ask and thou shalt receive'* business, if, when we do ask, we *don't* receive? It's not like I'm asking for the fucking world. I'd just like you to help out two very dear people. Is that *too* much to ask? I feel like Topol, in *'Fiddler on the roof '*. *'Would it spoil some vast, eternal plan............?'* What's the fucking point of it all? And no. I have no intention of apologizing for using the word *'fucking'*, twice in one paragraph. Correction. Make that, three times.

Before breakfast, I did my laundry and it is now laid out on the bed, airing and ready to be packed away.

The meal at Farmers last night was $11.94, plus a $2 tip. Really good value, and I would strongly recommend you pay the place a visit, sometime.

So, what am I going to do today? I have no idea.

10:05am. Is it too early to call Stella?

Early. Late. If she's not well, she's not well.

Oh, no! I've just realized. I'm not *supposed* to be writing. I'm *supposed* to be reading through all this rubbish and correcting the mistakes. Oh, Gawd. That's worse than having to write it.

Brendan J. A. O'Leary

Question: Do I relish the prospect of having to go through all this again next year?

Answer: *AAAAAAAAAAAAAAAAAAAAAARGH!*

I'll check my emails again. See if anyone loves me.

7:55am. I hate this part of the holiday. These last three days (back in Dickson) are always the worst. I must stress though, that this has absolutely nothing to do with the people of Dickson itself, who have shown me nothing but kindness in all the years I have been coming to this town.

Yesterday was a really bad day. I did very little. Oh, sure. It would be so easy to blame it on the weather. But, if I could have thought of something to do, or somewhere to go, then the cold and damp wouldn't have bothered me.

I guess I was feeling sorry for myself.

I tried calling a couple of friends, but all I got was voicemail and no one was calling me. I felt depressed, unloved and lonely. Yes. I even cried.

I spent most of yesterday in my room, staring blankly at the wall and imagining that I wasn't here, there or anywhere. Why do I keep putting myself through this? Hey! Haven't I written that before? Well, it certainly looks familiar to me.

Wouldn't you flaming well know it. The writer's block appears to have passed. Unfortunately, the only thing that's coming out is all this depressing shit.

On a lighter note. I have regained another penfriend. Yes folks. Although I managed to upset (and then lose) my two penfriends, fortunately, we have cleared the air and are once again communicating like civilized human beings. Isn't it nice when there's a happy ending?

Yes. I switched my computer on several times yesterday, in the vain hope that there would be a kindly message from someone, anyone, but message was there none. However, just before I went to bed, I thought I'd give it one last try, and lo and behold, there it was, a message from Hannah. Though I can't say for certain, it's probably the reason I slept so well. After all, my doctor did once tell me, *'Always go to bed with a happy thought in your mind'*. Yes. I know. It isn't always that easy. But, I'm sure you'll agree, that if we *could* all fall asleep with a happy thought in our minds, think how much better our sleep would be, and how much better we'd feel in the morning. Damn. I'm starting to sound like a counsellor, and I'm the one that needs it most. *'Where's my counsellor?'*

Of course, I also have a new friend here in Dickson to write to (Amanda) and, I'm going to write to Elaine, in Las Vegas.

All of a sudden, the dark cloud of depression that descended upon me and kept me cold and lonely is lifted and once again, I can bask in the warmth of the golden sun.

I saw a movie yesterday, *'The men who stare at goats'*. I went to the 4:25pm showing and, apart from myself, there was only one other person in there. Though it is a pretty good movie (and I would certainly recommend it), I would have enjoyed it more had I been in a better frame of mind. As with the last film I saw, I shall tell you nothing about it, just in case you want to see it for yourself. But! I will say this. *'The butler did it'*. Ha ha. Just a bit of earth humour there.

I had no dinner last night. I did, however, have a box of nachos, cheese and jalapenos, while watching the movie. Oh! And a Sprite. Not exactly health food, I know, but then, very little of what I eat whilst on holiday could be classed as health food. Except, that is, for the Raisin Bran. Can't get much healthier than that.

I guess I'll go and see Trudy this afternoon. No. Maybe I should leave it 'til this evening. What do you think? Oh, come on. Say something. I'm struggling here.

9:15am. It's about time I designed a cover for this......this...... whatever it is.

Thursday November 19th

8:20am. I'm late.

I've no idea what, if anything, there is to say.

I'll have to be out of here by 9:00am.

I saw Trudy yesterday. She tells me she *may* be pregnant. No! Of course it's not mine. But would it be such a bad thing if it were?

Trudy is now dating the guy she introduced me to before I started this road trip. At that time, they were just friends, but in the four weeks I was on the road their relationship has blossomed, and it may well be that Trudy has finally found someone decent. I hope so.

Last year, I came up with what I considered to be a pretty good ending for my journal. This year, I suspect it will end halfway through a sentence.

I desperately want to keep writing, though I have no idea what to say.

Perhaps I shall continue in the airport.

I'll catch you later.

11:00am. Damn! I'd written a couple of paragraphs, switched over to the Internet without saving said paragraphs, switched back and they'd gone.

Never mind. I was only talking about being in the airport, and trying to get hooked-up to the Internet. Hold on a sec. I'm just going to try something. No! Don't go! I'll be back shortly. Don't be so bloody impatient.

No. Didn't work.

I was just checking to see if I could send a conventional email, but no joy.

It doesn't matter. I just sent one via the Internet.

Strange that I haven't heard from Amanda. Ah. No worries. She'll get in touch when she's ready. She's probably a very busy woman.

These seats are bloody uncomfortable. They're made of metal, you know.

Why do I feel that there's something missing? I don't mean with me, you fool. I mean with the journal. I think we've already established that there is in fact, *a lot wrong with me*. I am, to put it mildly, *irreparably damaged*. Of course, I could be wrong. I've been wrong in the past. Hm. On many occasions, if I'm honest.

Isn't it wonderful to be able to plug your computer in at the airport? Well, these computers only have a three hour battery. Some days, it can take me longer than that to come up with anything of any interest to say.

Oh, Gawd. I'm starting to waffle. I'm doing another Victor Meldrew.

Still. Could be worse. Could be doing a Tony Hancock.

Oh, I don't know. Should I just write *'THE END'*, and have done with it?

Hey! I got my money back for that oil change I had done in Rapid City. $34.93. It all counts towards next year's spending money. *'From little acorns, great oaks do grow.'*

Maybe I'll do some more in Newark.

But! Should I fail to make it back home................. you'll just have to make up your own ending.

Hey! You know something? That's not such a bad idea. That way, everyone gets the ending they want, while I just ride off into the sunset on my post office bike. It's brilliant. Hell! I'm brilliant. I'd even go so far as to say, that I'm a legend in my own lounge. Or should that be, *'Airport Lounge'?*

5:30pm. Newark Airport, New Jersey.

Unfortunately, I cannot access the Internet in my present location, unless, that is, I am prepared to pay $9-95 per month. On discovering this, two words came into my head, and I'm pretty sure that you know what they were.

The flight from Nashville to Newark was delayed by one hour and forty minutes, though we only arrived in Newark an hour later than scheduled, as the pilot put the pedal to the metal, as it were.

We arrived in Newark at 4:30pm.

Not that that mattered, of course, as the flight to Manchester was not due to leave until 7:35pm.

Boarding went smoothly, on this final leg of my journey. Until, that is, it was discovered that one of the passengers was missing. No problem, you would think. No such luck. Unfortunately, the idiot (whoever he was) had checked his bags in, before mysteriously disappearing. This meant that his bag (bags) had to be located and then removed from the plane. Had it been my decision, I would have taken off with the bags on board. However, as we all know, it is a security risk.

We sat on the plane, at the gate, for over an hour, whilst they first unloaded all the bags and then reloaded them. It was soul-destroying.

I've said it before and I'll say it again: *'In my drinking days, I used to love flying.'* Now, however, it is nothing more than an imposition.

Sleep. What is sleep? I have enough trouble sleeping in a bed, so there is absolutely no chance of my sleeping on an aeroplane.

As on my outward-bound trip, my attempts at reading (what I have no doubt is yet another inspired piece of literature by the simply brilliant Stephen Fry) came to naught.

A thought has just occurred to me. *'The more I write, the more I have to correct.'*

So, it is with great sadness, that I utter these terminal words:

'THE END'